Wakefield Press

THE CASE FOR PALESTINE

Paul Heywood-Smith is an Australian barrister and Queen's Counsel who has maintained an interest in Palestine for over forty years. That interest led him to accept the role of Chairperson of the Australian Friends of Palestine Association, an organisation dedicated to the resolution of the Arab–Israeli conflict on the basis of international law and UN resolutions. He visited the West Bank and East Jerusalem in 2010 and has travelled widely in the neighbouring countries of Lebanon, Syria and Jordan.

The Case for Palestine

The Perspective of an Australian Observer

PAUL HEYWOOD-SMITH

Wakefield
Press

Wakefield Press
16 Rose Street
Mile End
South Australia 5031
www.wakefieldpress.com.au

First published 2014

Cover painting: *Jerusalem from the Austrian Hospice*,
painted by the author in 2010, kindly made available by
Dr Francis and Merlin Nathan.

Cover designed by Michael Deves, Wakefield Press
Edited by Julia Beaven, Wakefield Press
Text designed and typeset by Wakefield Press

National Library of Australia Cataloguing-in-Publication

Author:	Heywood-Smith, Paul, author.
Title:	The case for Palestine: the perspective of an Australian observer / Paul Heywood-Smith.
ISBN:	978 1 74305 330 0 (paperback).
Notes:	Includes bibliographical references and index.
Subjects:	Jewish–Arab relations.
	Arab–Israeli conflict.
	Palestine – Relations – Israel.
	Palestine – History.
Dewey Number:	956.94

fox creek
wines

CONTENTS

This book is dedicated to
Fathi Khalil Shahin,
and to his generation of Palestinians

Acronyms

AFOPA	Australian Friends of Palestine Association
AIPAC	American Israel Public Affairs Committee
BDS	Boycott Divestment Sanctions
CIA	Central Intelligence Agency
EU	European Union
HRW	Human Rights Watch
ICJ	International Court of Justice
IDF	Israeli Defense Forces
NGO	Non-Government Organisation
OECD	Organisation for Economic Co-operation and Development
PACs	Political Action Committees
PLO	Palestine Liberation Organization
UN	United Nations
UNRWA	United Nations Relief and Works Agency
USSR	Union of Soviet Socialist Republics

Foreword

The reader of Paul Heywood Smith's admirable overview of the Israel-Palestinian conflict should keep in mind that the struggle it describes is ongoing. The imbalance of power persists and so the disproportionate suffering of the Palestinians continues: illegal seizure of their land, destruction of their houses, daily shootings and arrests all go on apace.

As a consequence of this ongoing oppression the Israelis have succeeded in wearing down a portion of the Palestinian National Authority to the point where key leaders have capitulated and now cooperate with Israel in the suppression of resistance on the West Bank. Resistance coming from Gaza is more pronounced and usually takes the form of retaliatory missile attacks for Israeli border crossings and air strikes.

In order to move the balance of power in a direction more favourable to the Palestinians, the BDS (boycott, divestment and sanctions) movement has been developed. This movement is a worldwide one and is particularly active in Europe and the United States. It aims to isolate Israel economically and culturally by convincing those outside of Israel to have nothing to do with Israeli institutions and activities. The Israeli government now considers the BDS movement a major threat to the country's reputation and long term stability.

There is another aspect of this ongoing struggle that deserves mention. Israel claims to represent world Jewry. If the Israeli government can make this claim a true one it will have managed to tie an ancient religion to a modern secular and racist ideology. That ideology is Zionism, which calls for an exclusively Jewish state in Palestine and is the ideological basis for Israel's attempted ethnic cleansing of that territory. However, as yet Israel's claim of representation is not completely true.

An increasing number of the world's Jews find Israel's policies of ethnic cleansing and oppression to be appalling and have withdrawn their support for the Zionist state. Some have begun to ally with the Palestinians to resist Israeli ambitions.

Thus, the ongoing opposition to Israel is worldwide and very diversified. Palestinians now have allies among progressive Jews, Christians and Muslims. With patience and persistence, this is a struggle that can be won.

Lawrence Davidson

Lawrence Davidson is a retired professor of Middle East history. He is also an active public intellectual seeking to heighten awareness of the consequences of US policies in the Middle East.

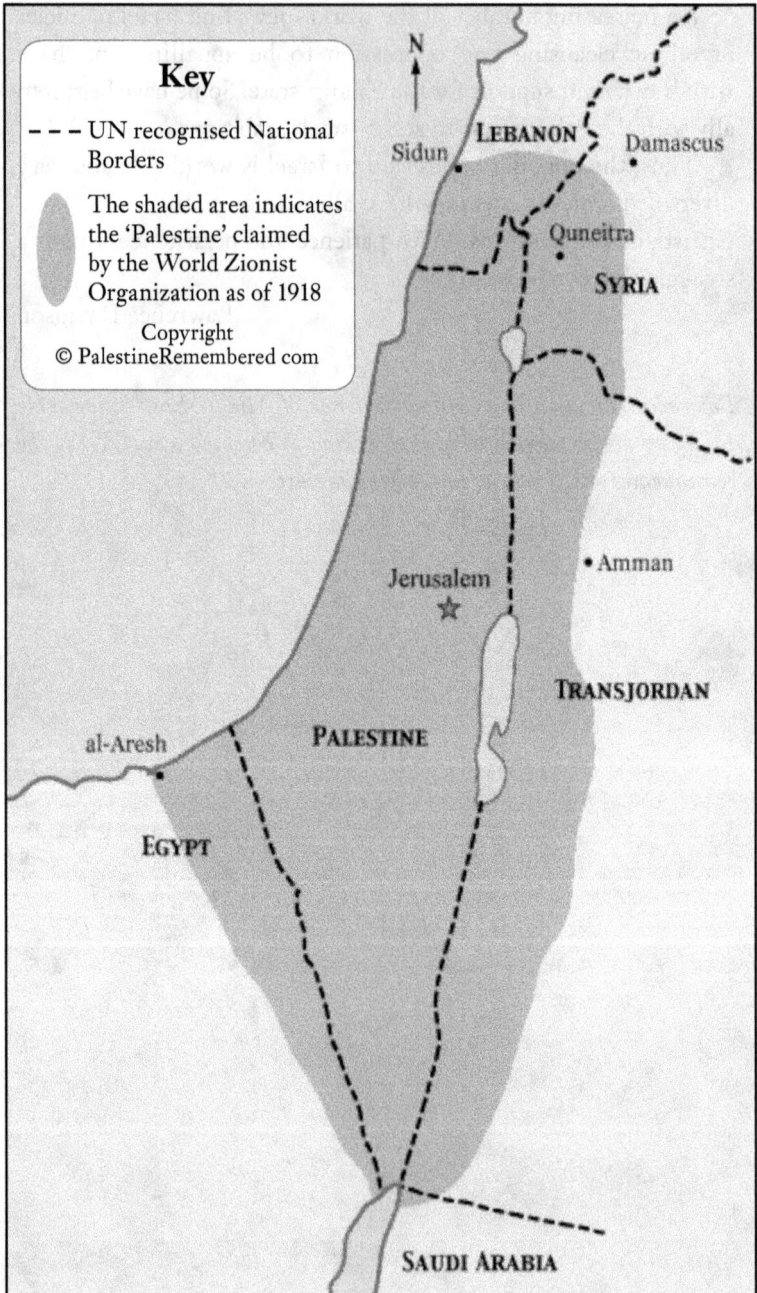

Key

- - - UN recognised National
Borders

The shaded area indicates
the 'Palestine' claimed
by the World Zionist
Organization as of 1918

Copyright
© PalestineRemembered com

N

LEBANON   Damascus

Sidun

Quneitra

SYRIA

Jerusalem
☆

• Amman

TRANSJORDAN

al-Aresh

PALESTINE

EGYPT

SAUDI ARABIA

Preface

Israel/Palestine is clearly one of the central issues of today's world. It has been for over 100 years. We cannot ignore this issue and also pretend to be concerned about the world or its people.

I am often asked, 'Why? Why are you, a white Anglo-Saxon male, of English and Anglican heritage, so interested in this issue?' The answer is that I fell into it. In 1973 I was a young, eager lawyer, in my first year of practice, as a solicitor at Lee Bolton & Lee, Solicitors, of 1 The Sanctuary, Westminster, in London. In the same year I enrolled in a course of International History in the 20th Century at the London School of Economics. October came and with it the Yom Kippur War. The newspapers were 100 per cent behind Israel. Everyone at the firm was 100 per cent behind Israel. My lecturer at the LSE was not, to the contrary. He asked the pertinent questions. He got me thinking.

On the following weekend I was in Hyde Park. I listened to a young man speaking on a soapbox. He said that he was an American, of Jewish origin. He was passing through London on his way to Israel to fight. He asserted that six million Jewish murders in the Holocaust meant that the world owed him and his brethren the State of Israel. I asked myself why. Certainly Germany and its satellites owed the Jewish people something. Some argued that the Allies could have done more to prevent the catastrophe. Perhaps they owed the Jewish people something. But why were the Palestinians obliged to give over their homes, their land, their olive groves, their lives, their culture, their country, their dignity, their *being*, for what was done by others? This was a question that I thought that Jewish people might understand.

I developed an interest that has turned into a lifelong passion. It has impacted on my life in many ways – not all beneficial. I have, however, no regrets.

This small book – some would say polemic but I prefer book – is the result of being asked to give a series of lectures in Adelaide, South Australia, to the University of the Third Age. In compiling the lectures, I have relied to some degree on earlier speeches I gave in my then position as Chairperson of the Australian Friends of Palestine Association.

It is also the result of my perception that an accessible book of modest size and ambition is required amidst the vast array of serious (and lengthy) academic works. Necessarily, such a book has its limitations. Any purported account of over 2000 years of history in around 100 pages is in danger of seriously distorting by summary.

I am not a historian. I am a lawyer. I apologise if I appear to cite legal authority too often. If lawyers do anything well it is to assemble in logical form other people's work. I have read widely from a range of sources. If I am accused of plagiarism, I will probably have to plead guilty. I have freely adopted the ideas of others where I thought they were accurate or interesting.

I am clearly partisan. However, to the extent that I consider consistent with truth, I have attempted to be fair. Some will consider that I have failed in that endeavour – from both sides.

There is one matter I have noted. Something new happens almost every day. In the event I have developed a sense of urgency over publication. The finished book is, I can confidently assert, as up to date as it could possibly be.

I have attempted to reference my assertions. Some will note that I have not been able to – or simply have not, in some instances. This is no doubt the result of expressing my beliefs. That is something that I will have to live with. I stand by my beliefs however.

Preface

I commence with a quote from Edward Said's testimony to the US Congressional Subcommittee on International Relations in 1975.

Imagine to yourselves that by some malicious irony you found yourselves declared foreigners in your own country. This is the essence of the Palestinian's fate during the 20th century.

Paul Heywood-Smith, 2014

CHAPTER 1

Ancient History and Religion

The history of Palestine is inseparable from a history of three of the great religions: Judaism, Christianity and Islam. It will be necessary to consider them and their differences, including internal differences. But let us start with the land.

The land that is Palestine is an ancient land where humans have lived continuously for at least 9000 years. It is in that part of the world known as 'the cradle of civilisation'. At no time, certainly in the last 3500 years, did people cease to live there. The Zionist catch-cry 'A land without a people for a people without a land' was, when first uttered in the 19th century, palpably wrong.

Of course, 2000 years ago there was not a land with geographical borders known as Palestine, or any other name, pertaining to that piece of geography that we know today. The nation state is of course a substantially 19th century creation. This idea is most clearly understood when one considers the modern state of Germany, which did not come together as a nation state until the late 19th century.

In biblical times, which can be interpreted as anything from 1000 BCE (Before the Current Era) to 400 CE (Current Era), people of the Jewish faith, and others – then called Jebusites, Philistines, Canaanites, Moabites, Edomites, people who we today call Arabs – lived in Palestine, then known as the Land of Canaan. Purists might say that the only pure Arabs in Palestine in biblical times were the nomadic Bedouin.

It should also be understood that people of the Jewish faith lived far wider afield than the area we now know as Palestine. Jewish communities existed in the seaports of the Mediterranean, retaining a sense of identity to each other and to Jerusalem. The largest was Alexandria, said to have as many as a million Jews by the time of Jesus's coming.

Palestine was ruled by everyone and anyone in the neighbourhood – Egyptians, Assyrians, Babylonians, Syrians, Persians, and Romans. It became part of the Roman Empire in 63 BCE, when Pompey imposed Roman rule. For something approaching 80 years prior to that time there had been what might be described as a form of independent Jewish state, at least in part of Palestine (particularly Jerusalem and its environs to the north and south), known as Judea. It was not to be for two millennia that another state calling itself a Jewish state would exist in Palestine. It is significant to note however that the 'state' was not more than a community. There were other communities occupying the same space we today call Palestine. The Samaritans were another such community occupying the district of Palestine known as Samaria. Samaritanism is a separate Abrahamic religion albeit closely related to Judaism. Most Samaritans converted to Islam in the 8th century CE.

It is appropriate to say something of the life of Christ. King Herod, who reigned from 37 BCE to 4 BCE and built the Second Temple, was half Jew and half Arab. Antipater, his father, was an Edomite or Idumean who converted to Judaism. His mother Cyprus was a Nabatean princess. In the event he was Jewish, in part, it was only by religion. It is a pity that he is not celebrated today. Christ of course was a Jew.

It would appear that Jesus through his teachings and actions, particularly in the Temple, was seen to challenge the established order (with some apparent success evidenced by public sympathy). That established order saw a powerful group of Jews, influential men of standing in the community, use their position to secure Roman support. In other words Jesus is seen more as a political threat to the established order, rather than a theological challenge to that order.

Jesus is arrested by the captain of the Temple, a Jew. The chief priests take Jesus to Pilate and negotiate his execution. He is then executed by the Romans as a criminal. This occurs quickly; Jesus is apparently arrested one day and executed the next. There is some evidence to suggest that it was more convenient for Christians seeking to establish their religion within the Roman Empire to downplay the responsibility of Pontius Pilate – thus the 'washing of the hands' narrative.

The followers of Christ – Christians – claimed to be the true heirs of the Old Testament, a claim, of course, which aroused concern amongst Jews.

Something needs to be said of 'the Temple'. It is 'per se' a concept of immense importance to all religious Jews. Tradition has it that King David (circa 1000 BCE) placed the Ark of the Covenant on Mount Moriah, one of the two mountains of Jerusalem, and it was there that his son Solomon built the First Temple in 960 BCE. The First Temple was destroyed by the Babylonians in 587 BCE. The Second Temple was built in 520 BCE. It existed for about 600 years until it was burned by the Romans in 70 CE. In 70 CE Titus put down a rebellion and in doing so destroyed the Temple. It was never to be rebuilt. The Jewish communities of Palestine were substantially reduced in significance by Syrian and Greek veterans of Titus's legions. Sixty years later Hadrian effectively wiped Judea off the map renaming it Palaestina, after the Philistines. This campaign put down what is known as the Bar Kokhba Revolt, named after its leader Simon Bar Kokhba. Jerusalem was re-named Aelia Capitolina and Jews forbidden from living there.

Most of the Jewish population was enslaved following the Bar Kokhba Revolt and dispersed throughout the Empire, particularly the Mediterranean basin and lands adjoining the Black Sea. The Jewish population of Europe and North Africa was reinforced from this stock. Some communities of Jewish people remained in Palestine and its immediate environs. However the Jewish religion lost its driving power there and, as the centuries passed, the remaining Jewish communities became of lesser significance. There were 43 Jewish communities there in the 6th century.

One major factor in this process was Constantine becoming Emperor in 306 CE. He was to make the momentous decision of adopting Christianity as one of the religions for the Empire. Galerius had issued the Edict of Tolerance in 311 CE. After Constantine I became sole emperor, he issued the Edict of Milan in 313 CE. It was not until the 380s, under Theodosius, that Christianity became the state religion of the Empire and paganism was outlawed.

Thus it was that the 4th century resulted in Jerusalem becoming a Christian city – aided by Constantine's mother, Helena. Shlomo Sand, in his recent book *The Invention of the Land of Israel*, notes that from 135 BCE to the mid-19th century some 30 Jewish texts of pilgrimages to the Holy Land by Jews were recorded. In the same period there are 3500 documented reports of Christian pilgrimages.[1]

With the fall of the Roman Empire, Palestine came to be ruled by Persia and Byzantium. In 638 CE Jerusalem surrendered to the Arab Caliphate. Whilst Muslims, Jews and Christians have all resided in Palestine, there can be no doubt that the substantial, if not overwhelming majority, were Muslim and Arab from that time until today.

It is also important to note this. The indigenous peoples of Canaan/Palestine were constantly being invaded, situated, as the land was, at a crossroads. It is natural that those indigenous peoples took on the different religions, cultures and customs of each new wave of invaders. The vast bulk of the indigenous peoples never left the land. The Palestinians of the 20th century claimed Palestine simply by reason of the fact that they were the indigenous inhabitants from time immemorial. Theirs was the same claim as all other peoples of the world to their land of habitation.

This is as good a place as any to consider the difference between the three religions of the Book. Judaism is the oldest of the monotheistic religions. Its story is that of the Old Testament.

Judaism's creed is based on the concept of the omnipotent One True God whose will is revealed in the *Torah*, the first five books of the Old Testament. The One True God has a special relationship with his 'Chosen People'. The *Torah* was divinely revealed to Moses on Mount Sinai soon after the exodus of the Israelites from Egypt in the 13th century BCE. Judaism rejected the concept of the Incarnation and hence Jesus was not recognised as the Messiah. Judaism was affected by the Enlightenment in Europe in the 18th century. A 'reform' Judaism developed; but the orthodox Jew remained, and the associated strict observances of all aspects of daily life are still a feature of orthodoxy, and indeed created tension between orthodox, reform and particularly secular Jews.

Judaism was the parent of both Christianity and Islam. Christianity is based on the life of Jesus whose teachings are found in the New Testament's four gospels of Matthew, Mark, Luke and John. But Christianity sought to incorporate the Old Testament into its story. And of the Jews, Christianity took the position that unless baptised, they lost their place in the kingdom of Christ and God. Through unbelief they were broken off.

Like Judaism, Christianity did not remain a single whole faith. The Eastern Church of Byzantine Europe from the 5th century BCE differed in various ways from the Western Church. The centre of the Eastern Church was Constantinople (Istanbul) whilst that of the Western Church was Rome. By the 11th century the breach between the Catholic and Orthodox was permanent. The Reformation in the 16th century in turn breached the unity of the Catholic Church. Protestantism gave the right to each man to interpret the scriptures in his own way. Today, the ecumenical movement promotes the reunion of Christendom.

Islam was founded in the 7th century CE by the prophet Mohammed. Mohammed invoked the Old Testament and claimed to be a successor to Moses. He recognised Jesus as a prophet. Islam rejected the Christian doctrine of the Incarnation and Trinity but the Muslims regard their religion as completing and perfecting those of the other People of the Book – the Jews and Christians – who they believed to have gone astray or misunderstood God's message as transmitted to them through Moses and Jesus.

The sacred book of Islam is the Koran (Qur'an) the words of which were revealed to Mohammed by Allah through the agency of the angel Gabriel, first in Mecca and later in Medina. Like orthodox Judaism, Islam is a literal-minded religion indicating the everyday duties of the believer.

As with Christianity Islam did not remain a united religion. Shortly after the death of Mohammed, feuding ensued over the succession. The orthodox, Sunnites, or Sunni Muslims, selected Omar, an advisor to Mohammed. The Shi'ites, or Shia, maintained that Ali, the Prophet's son-in-law, husband of His daughter Fatima, was the true successor to the Prophet. The centre of the Shia sect is based in Persia (today's Iran). The orthodox Sunni are the majority throughout the Middle East. It is estimated that 65 per cent of Muslims in the Middle East are Sunni and 30 per cent Shia. Shi'ites and Sunni recognise each other as Muslims adhering to the five pillars of the faith. To the outsider there would appear to be no basis for bloodshed between the two.

The writer recalls his childhood in Australia in the 1950s. At that time a clear line divided the Catholic and Protestant communities. Today, my children would laugh at the suggestion of a difference. Perhaps some similar advance awaits the two major sects of Islam. Unfortunately one cannot see any basis for optimism that such an eventuality might occur.

There then are the three religions of the Book. One can only reflect upon how prophetic was Lucretius, who lived in the century before the current era (BCE). Lucretius asserts: *tantum religio potuit suadere malorum* (so great is the power of religion to lead us to evil).

And so to the evil.

'God gave us this land.'

'I give this country to your posterity from the river of Egypt up to the Great River, Euphrates': Genesis XV, verse 18.

For the Jews this is the origin of their right to the Promised Land. However the 'posterity' includes the descendants of Ishmael since he was the son of Abraham by his concubine Ketivah, and the ancestor of all the Arabs, Christian or Muslim.

I.F. Stone, 'Holy War'

As indicated, for some 80 years there was a Jewish 'state' in Palestine before the birth of Christ. Should any weight be given to that as a claim by the Jewish peoples to Palestine? Why would weight not be given to an Italian claim, the Romans having ruled in Palestine for half a millennium; or to a French claim, Frankish Christians having ruled in the Holy Land in the 12th and 13th centuries?

And what of the Palestinian peoples themselves, they having existed in Palestine in one form or another as a Muslim State for centuries before the Crusades and 700 years after? Nor could today's Palestinians be divorced from the ancient tribes of Israel. Over 2000 years Jews and Christians have converted to Islam either through intermarriage or encouragement and necessarily joined with and become of one blood: what we call Palestinians today.

But in any event one might like to ask, whose God? If you believe in God, is not the God of the Jews, the Christians, and the Muslims the same God? Are not the Jews, the Christians and the Muslims the peoples of the same Book?

Modern Zionists attempt to be a little more subtle than relying directly upon the Book of Genesis. Simon Schama, the historian, criticising Shlomo Sand's *The Invention of the Jewish People*[2] asserted that the book 'fails to sever the remembered connection between the ancestral land and Jewish experience'. Whatever that means, why could the same not be asserted of Christian and Muslim experience?

This chapter commenced with the Zionist slogan 'A land without a people for a people without a land'. For an Australian of British ancestry such a slogan necessarily touches a raw or sensitive chord. Australia was of course described as 'terra nullius'. No doubt a myriad of arguments can be advanced to distinguish the two scenarios. That genocide was practised on the Australian aboriginal cannot be denied. Readers interested in attempts by Australia to rectify the wrong might well start with the decision of the Australian High Court in Mabo and Another v The State of Queensland [1988] 166 CLR 186 and Mabo (No. 2) (1992) 175 CLR 1. The result of that case was 'that the common law of this country recognises a form of native title'.[3]

CHAPTER 2

The 7th to the 19th Century

At the end of the 7th century the Caliph (successor to the Prophet), Abd-al Malik, built the Dome of the Rock on the Temple Mount. The skyline of Jerusalem was thereafter seized to this day by Islam. Then, in the 8th century, the Muslim people of Palestine built the Al-Aqsa Mosque in Jerusalem. The Temple Mount was turned by the caliphs into a holy Islamic shrine. Christians had the Church of the Holy Sepulchre. Jerusalem was at this time overwhelmingly Christian, but Muslims and Christians mixed freely. Many Christians were led to convert to Islam by the dhimmi tax or tribute, payable by non-Muslims for the right of residence in Jerusalem.

It is ironic today that because of the easy-going tolerance of the Arabs, the Jews found almost complete religious freedom under the Arabian caliphs. Although persecuted in Europe, for a thousand years the Jews throughout the Middle East, Maghrev and Iberia lived at peace with their neighbours. No clearer example of this exists than the way that the Jews welcomed the Moorish invaders of Spain in the eighth century as liberators. Jews had lived in Spain since the destruction of the Second Temple but had been subjected to persecution. The Jews became the allies of the invading Arabs, becoming administrators in the new society.

There is as well considerable evidence that the Ashkenazi Jew, as opposed to the Sephardic Jew, is substantially derived from the conversion of the Khazars to Judaism in or about 805 CE. The Khazars were Turkish nomads who occupied that land between the Black and Caspian seas (called the Caucasus today), including parts of eastern Turkey, north-west Iran and Georgia. Khazaria seems the likely source of the Jewish influx into Russia, the Ukraine,

Poland, and Eastern Europe – and from there, into Western Europe. 'Ashkenaz' is the Hebrew name for Germany. Yiddish, the Ashkenazi language, which is written in Hebrew characters, is a 13th century German vernacular.

The Sephardic Jew, strictly, designates Jews whose ancestors came from the Iberian Peninsula. 'Sepharad' means 'Spain' in Hebrew. In a general sense, today, however, Sephardic Jews are those Jews whose roots are around the Mediterranean, the Middle East, and Asia. When speaking of 'around the Mediterranean' the intention is to exclude anything north of the Pyrenees and the Caucasus. Ashkenazi culture is North European and Slavic, Sephardic culture is predominantly Mediterranean and Middle Eastern. This might be said of the Sephardic Jews. They lived in the Islamic world. They did so as one of several religious and ethnic minorities. They integrated into society, spoke Arabic, and identified with the same culture and way of life.

The Ashkenazi today outnumber the Sephardic Jew some ten to one. Thus the great bulk of what we call the Jewish race today, and which also form the Jewish inhabitants of Israel, may not be the descendants of a biblical tribe from Palestine. The term 'race' is problematic. The word 'people' must be more appropriate.[1] It is difficult to see how the term 'race' is appropriate when people might convert, and of course have converted, to Judaism as a religion.

Writers from Arthur Koestler, *The Thirteenth Tribe*, 1976, to the more recent Shlomo Sand in *The Invention of the Jewish People* have claimed that much of European Jewry are actually descended from these Turkic tribesmen, the Khazars. *If true, this would undermine Zionism.* When Sand, as an Israeli Jew, was asked if he was saying that the true descendants of the inhabitants of the Kingdom of Judah are the Palestinians, he responded: 'No population remains pure over a period of thousands of years. But the chances that the Palestinians are the descendants of the ancient Judaic people are much greater than the chances that you or I (Ashkenazi Jews) are its descendants.'

The writer adds, so as not to be exclusive or elitist, that the chances of his having pure Anglo-Saxon blood, without any Semitic blood, must be similarly remote.

Montefiore in his history *Jerusalem*[2], notes Koestler and Sand but asserts that modern genetics substantially refutes their claims, suggesting that only 30 per cent of today's Jews descend from European as opposed to Middle Eastern stock. No references are however given by Montefiore. And nor does Montefiore say what he means by 'Middle Eastern' stock. Does Middle Eastern include the Khazars?

From the 10th century onwards, the majority of the world's Jewry was settled in Europe, and became, decisively, a European, as opposed to an Oriental or Near Eastern people. This is critical, because it meant that when the Jews 'returned' at the end of the 19th and beginning of the 20th centuries, they did so as colonisers.

In the 12th and 13th centuries, following the capture of Jerusalem in 1099 by the Crusaders, Christians generally ruled in Palestine, in what might be called feudal estates, or fiefdoms, rather than as a country. The city was purged of its Muslim and Jewish inhabitants by the orgy of killing following its capture.

We should not fail to understand the Crusades and their importance to us today. The Crusades were the then 'West' (the Holy Roman Empire, the Franks), seeking to secure the Holy Land for Christianity. It is very little different to today's 'West' – the US and Europe – propping up Zionism in apparent opposition to Islam.

At the end of the 12th century, Saladin expelled the crusaders and Jerusalem became an Islamic city again. He in turn was challenged by Richard the Lionheart and an arm wrestle ensued, between Christian and Muslim. Frederick II regained Jerusalem by treaty in 1229 CE.

The 13th to 16th centuries saw Palestine ruled by the Mamluks – a Turkish Master class – Islamic, but nevertheless

Christians and Jews were tolerated. Montefiore asserts that in the 15th century there was a community of Jews in Jerusalem living in what became the Jewish Quarter. They were outnumbered many fold by Christian and Muslim inhabitants.

From the 16th to 20th centuries, Palestine was a part of the Ottoman Empire. For those who consider that the world does not change much it is of interest to note that between 1534 and 1553 Suleiman conducted three campaigns against Persia. Persia was Turkey's traditional enemy, not only in national but in religious terms, since the Turks were orthodox Sunni and the Persians heterodox Shia.

At the start of the Ottoman Empire, in the mid-16th century, Suleiman the Magnificent restored and redecorated the Dome of the Rock. In Suleiman's time the population of Jerusalem was 16,000 of whom 2000 were Jews. The descendants of those 14,000 non-Jews – Christians and Muslims – assuredly include the million Arabs living in Palestine in 1948.

But the 15th and 16th centuries also saw the expulsion of tens of thousands of Jews from Ferdinand and Isabella's Spain. The expulsion order was made in 1492. The expulsion was of all Jews who did not convert to Christianity. They, the Sephardim, fled eastward to the Ottoman Empire where they were welcomed by the then Sultan, Suleiman the Magnificent, and to the Balkans and Anatolia, to Istanbul, Salonica (now Thessaloniki), Rhodes and Jerusalem. The Ottoman Empire became the home of the Sephardic Jew.

A current development is of interest. In February 2014 the Spanish government approved a draft bill to allow descendants of those Sephardic Jews so expelled to seek dual citizenship, that is, with Spain and the country of present residence. The proposed law is said to apply to an estimated 3.5 million persons presently living in Israel, the United States, France, Turkey, Mexico, Argentina and Chile.

∞※∞

The Ottoman period saw the ascendancy, so far as the Christian third of the equation, of the Armenians (who were Orthodox Christians) opposed to the Catholics. But the Armenians were Ottomans as much as Christians. They remained Ottomans until 1915 when, as the Ottoman Empire's Christian minority, they were 'cleansed' from the Empire in what is today widely considered to be an act of genocide.

A reminder of the Armenians exists in the form of the Armenian Quarter in Old Jerusalem today – perceived perhaps by the 21st-century visitor (at least the Western one) as an oddity or anachronism.

It is appropriate to record the Crimean War, which commenced in 1853, following Napoleon III's attempt to embrace Levantine Christians in 1852. That attempt was no doubt the cause of Czar Nicholas I's attempt to pressure the Ottomans over primacy in Jerusalem, that is, primacy of the Orthodox Church over the Latin Church. In practical terms primacy meant, inter alia, whether the Latin monks, to pass through the Church of the Nativity into their grotto, should possess a key to its chief door, together with one of the keys to each of the two doors of the manger itself. Today this might seem a triviality, but it must be noted that also at stake was the grant of a Russian protectorate over the Greek Orthodox subjects of the Ottoman Empire.

The British and French declared war on Russia. This was the time when the Ottoman Empire was perceived to be in serious decline. The British and French were anxious that Russia not pick up the spoils. Even though the fighting occurred in the Crimea, it should not be forgotten that Jerusalem was the (Tsar's) object, and from then on Jerusalem and Palestine have remained at the centre of the world stage.

Today Palestine *is* the world stage, pulling in to it all of its offshoots – Egypt, Jordan, Lebanon, Syria, Iraq, Iran, Afghanistan, Somalia, the US, Europe, Australia …

It should be recognised that the decline of the Ottoman Empire had its own impact on the Jewish communities within that Empire. They too declined. The impetus to convert to Islam was intensified. The Ottoman Jews fell behind their Western European brothers and sisters.

⌘

It is of interest to note the role of Benjamin Disraeli. Disraeli was of Italian–Jewish ancestry. His father converted Benjamin to Christianity as a child. Disraeli did not however give up his attachment to the Jewish peoples and his recognised intellectual attachment to the Holy Land. He promoted British ties with Asia. It was he who, as prime minister, through his connections with the Rothschilds, secured for Britain a major interest in 1875 in the Suez Canal. This was Britain's first tangible entry into the Middle East, rendering Egypt and Palestine strategic objects of great import.

By the 1880s Palestine was peopled by 650,000 (mostly Arab) peoples. No more than 50,000 of this population were of the Jewish faith. People of the Jewish faith lived around the world – as Russians, Poles, Austro-Hungarians, Germans, French, British, American, Australian, Turkish, Moroccan, Tunisian, Persian, Greek peoples – practising their religion as citizens of those countries, their countries. But not all assimilated well. I say that not in a critical way. Much of the withdrawal of the Jewish faith into itself might be said to be the result of the determination of the ascendant Christian religion (particularly at the end of the Roman Empire) to distance itself from its parent, and impose constraints upon it.

By the late 19th century, anti-Semitism was a fact of life in many European countries, as evidenced, for example, by the Dreyfus affair in France and the pogroms in Russia.

It is necessary to spend a moment on the term 'anti-Semitism'. It is an emotive and provocative term. A 'Semite' is defined as a member of any of the peoples supposed to be descended from Shem, son of Noah. This includes the Jews, Arabs, Assyrians, Babylonians and Phoenicians. More generally Semitic peoples might be considered as of Near Eastern origin. So that when the term 'anti-Semitism' is used it might be expected that one is speaking of dislike or contrariness towards people form the Near East.

That is not, however, how the term has come to be used. Rather, over the last 100 to 150 years it has come to be used as a euphemism for 'Judeophobia', hatred of Jews because they are Jews.

In the context of the Ashkenazi/Sephardic divide the phrase is thrown into relief. Sephardic Jews are clearly Semites. Not so readily are the Ashkenazim perceived to be Semites. But the utility of the term 'anti-Semitism' to the Zionists is apparent. If used in respect of all Jews, including the Ashkenazim, it suggests that all Jews are Semitic, that is of Near Eastern origin, belonging in the Near East, and naturally disposed, indeed having a right, to return to their origins.

⁂

Let us return then to Dreyfus. Dreyfus was a Jewish officer in the French Army who was falsely accused of passing military secrets to the Germans. The case was based around the forged evidence of a slip of paper found in a waste-paper basket. Thus framed by government officials as a traitor, anti-Semitism was raised to a national passion. National security was invoked to cover up the crime of the true culprit, Major Esterhazy, and as exposure loomed the government was threatened. It became more and more apparent that France's honour itself was at stake. The affair lasted some 12 years, during which France and particularly Paris were totally polarised. Justice was ultimately to triumph.

Alexander III of Russia regarded the Jews as a social cancer, worthy of persecution by honest Orthodox Russians. His May Laws of 1882 made anti-Semitism state policy. It resulted in mass migration of Jews from Russia – 85 per cent to America.

It is appropriate too to mention a curious document, 'The Protocols of the Elders of Zion'. Evidence suggests that at or about the beginning of the 20th century the Tsarist government in

Russia prepared this document in an attempt to stave off all reform. The document, prepared in an office maintained by Russia's police in Paris, purported to be a series of lectures describing how Jews would overthrow all Gentile governments and replace them with a Jewish world empire. Thus any threat of change was presented as a Jewish manoeuvre. Unsurprisingly, following the Russian Revolution, the document gained some measure of credence given the prominence of Kerensky, and then Trotsky and other Jewish Bolsheviks.

$$\infty\!\!\!\infty$$

But why anti-Semitism? Presumably it started from the fact that the Jews had rejected Jesus of Nazareth as the Messiah. Even worse, they had killed him, and not repented after His resurrection. Matthew sets the scene for what is to come: Pilate

> washed his hands before the multitude saying, I am innocent of the blood of this just person ...

> Then answered all the people, and said. His blood be on us and on our children. Matthew 27.24, 25

To be sure that the record, so far as anyone can know it, is however clear, it is appropriate to note that it is only Matthew of the four gospel writers who asserts this.

This early allocation of blame was apparently compounded when European Christendom turned every civic act into a religious ceremony. Citizenship became a matter of baptism and marriage – even death – within the Christian Church. The Jew was excluded. He was barred from political responsibility. Denied land tenure and access to artisan and commercial guilds he was less to European society than the Palestinian is in Israel today. His permission to reside in any city or state was at the discretion of the ruling king or prince. The privilege in time came at a price, princes relying upon resident Jews as a source of income. Indeed, they were relied upon as financial advisers and agents to the princes – 'court Jews'.

The reputation as usurer grew, bringing with it the enmity of the good Christian. Shylock entered the common consciousness. Reacting, Judaism became less tolerant but more insecure, driving communities within the walls of their houses, the shtetl, and thence into the ghetto, which in time became their compulsory residence. The Jews became obsessed with their mythical past, men escaped to religious study, and minutiae of ritual took on greater and greater importance, as did the position of the rabbi. The Jew became the alien, whilst other ethnic groups – Syrians, Greeks, Italians – Christians all, were absorbed into northern European society.

Shakespeare informs. *The Merchant of Venice* is dated between 1594 and 1598. The barest of plots has Antonio, the rich Venetian merchant, borrowing 3000 ducats from Shylock, the money-lending Jew, in order to loan the monies to his friend Bassanio to enable him to seek the hand of Portia. Shylock bears a grudge against Antonio for the Christian's prior treatment of him and attaches to the loan the bond of losing 'a pound of flesh' if the money is not paid within three months. Antonio's ships are reported lost and the three months pass. Shylock will not accept the monies from another. Portia makes her plea and Shylock is caught by her demand that Shylock not cut more or less than an exact pound, for if he does, he must lose all his goods and be put to death.

Along the way Shakespeare weaves his magic, enabling us to look into the 16th-century mind. He does this through the words of Shylock himself:

> How like a fawning publican he looks!
> I hate him for he is a Christian,
> But more for that in low simplicity
> He lends out money gratis and brings down
> The rate of usance here with us in Venice.
> If I can catch him once upon the hip,
> I will feed fat the ancient grudge I bear him.

He hates our sacred nation, and he rails,
Even there where merchants most do congregate,
On me, my bargains and my well won thrift,
Which he calls interest. Cursed be my tribe,
If I forgive him!
Act I, Scene iii

Signor Antonio, many a time and oft
In the Rialto you have rated me
About my moneys and my usances:
Still have I borne it with a patient shrug,
For sufferance is the badge of all our tribe.
You call me misbeliever, cut-throat dog,
And spit upon my Jewish gabardine,
And all for use of that which is mine own.
Act I, Scene iii

Hath not a Jew eyes? hath not a Jew hands, organs,
dimensions, senses, affections, passions? fed with the same
food, hurt with the same weapons, subject to the same
diseases, healed by the same means, warmed and cooled
by the same winter and summer, as a Christian is? If you
prick us, do we not bleed? if you tickle us do we not laugh?
if you poison us, do we not die? and if you wrong us, shall
we not revenge? If we are like you in the rest, we will
resemble you in that.
Act III, Scene i

And how does it end? Why Antonio shows mercy. Portia
claims that having made an attempt on the life of a citizen, a half
of Shylock's goods goes to the injured man, the other half to the
state, and his life itself is at the mercy of the duke. The duke gives
Shylock his life and Antonio begs the duke to allow the Jew to
keep half his property on condition that he gives the other half
to Antonio in trust for Shylock's daughter *and on condition that
he at once becomes a Christian.* Shylock agrees and leaves the court

indisposed. To the reader from the 21st century this surely grates. That reader must have sympathy for Theodor Herzl, the founder of Zionism, and wonder why he did not act sooner.

It is of interest to the Australian observer, of British ancestry, to consider the position in England. The Jews are mentioned in Magna Carta (para. 10). The clause relates to usury upon debts owed to the Jews. The Jews were expelled by Edward I in 1290 and returned following the Restoration in the 17th century. Thereafter they suffered no more disability than other non-conformists to the established Church.[3] The principal nonconformists were of course the Papists; there were no Muslim communities for comparison.

That is not to say that there was no disability facing the Jews. As Blackstone recorded: 'Christianity is part of the law of England.'[4] In *Traske's Case* (1618) Hob. 236, the Star Chamber sentenced the accused for maintaining that the Jewish and not the Christian Sabbath should be observed, and that pork should be avoided. The preaching of these opinions tended 'to sedition' and scandalised the king, bishops and clergy.[5]

Blackstone, writing in 1769, also notes 'that Jews, and other infidels and heretics, were not capable of the benefit of clergy till after the Statute 5 Ann. C6' (1707).[6] The 'benefit of clergy' was the immunity of churchmen (clerics) from the temporal courts – they, rather, were subject to the canon law.

The Toleration Act of 1689 was directed to Protestant non-conformists. It guaranteed religious freedom, but with qualifications. Anglicans were privileged; certain offices, both of state and in the universities, were reserved for them. But Protestants who could bring themselves to occasionally take the Anglican communion got by, and in London some Jews even held local government office.

An Act of 1753 sought to legalise the naturalisation of Jews. However it brought anti-Semitic mobs on to the streets of London and was immediately repealed. It was not until 1846 (9, 10 Victoria, c.59) that Jews were finally relieved of their disabilities. With respect to their schools, synagogues and charities they were put on the same footing as Protestant nonconformists.

Between 1880 and 1930 there was a massive influx of Jews from Russia and Poland. These Ashkenazim overwhelmed the established Sephardim in English society.

⚛️

Anti-Semitism was the inspiration for Theodor Herzl (who perchance had been the Paris correspondent for an Austrian newspaper which reported on the Dreyfus affair) to commence the Zionist movement to create a home for the Jewish people in Palestine. Some might say a noble goal, but for the fact that the plan, as evidenced by Herzl's diary, was that it was to be at the expense of the native population who were to be spirited out of the country and their land expropriated.[7]

Compare however the anti-Semitism of Europe with the position in then Palestine. Montefiore writes this as a description of a multicultural Jerusalem in the late 19th century:

> During the Jewish festival of Purim, Muslim and Christian Arabs dressed up in the traditional Jewish costumes, and all three religions attended the Jewish Picnic held at the tomb of Simon the Just north of the Damascus Gate. Jews presented their Arab neighbours with matzah and invited them to the Passover Seder dinner, while the Arabs returned the favour by giving the Jews newly baked bread when the festival ended. Jewish mohels often circumcised Muslim children. Jews held parties to welcome their Muslim neighbours back from the haj. The closest relations were between Arabs and Sephardic Jews ... Ironically, the Arab Orthodox Christians were the most hostile to Jews, whom they insulted in traditional Easter songs and lynched as they approached the Church.

It is appropriate to acknowledge this. For 2000 years Jews had related themselves to Jerusalem. They prayed towards Jerusalem, wished each other 'Next year in Jerusalem' every year at Passover. But could similar sentiments not be said of both Christians and Muslims, and just as strongly?

The connection of Christians to Jerusalem is obvious:

Jerusalem is where it all happened. It is the site of the Church of the Holy Sepulchre. The connection of Muslims must similarly be accepted. It is the site of the Al-Aqsa Mosque, an Islamic holy place. It is said to be named Al-Aqsa by God. A chapter of the Koran, entitled 'The Night Journey', describes the transporting of the apostle of God, Mohammed, from Medina to Jerusalem, where He prayed with Abraham and Moses.

It is also appropriate to acknowledge this. There are no absolutes. Many good and worthy Jewish immigrants no doubt came to Palestine in the 50 years preceding WW II and after. Not all were Zionists. They were people looking for a home. They are today perhaps the people who have ended up on the wrong side of history.

CHAPTER 3

Early 20th Century and the Balfour Declaration

And so the Zionist movement commenced to buy Arab land in Palestine and encouraged Jews to go there. A wave of Russian Jews escaping more Tsarist persecution arrived in the early 1900s.

The Jewish National Fund, established in 1901, laid down that all land that it acquired was to remain inalienable Jewish property that could not be sold or leased to others. This is so even today. Moreover, when circumstances allowed, only Jews should work the land that Jews acquired.

The movement had friends in high places. Dr Chaim Weizmann – a Russian-born scientist – became an insider in Whitehall. He was later to become the first president of the State of Israel. He had the ear of David Lloyd-George and Arthur Balfour. Lloyd-George became prime minister in 1916 and appointed Balfour his foreign secretary.

Thus we are led to the Balfour Declaration in 1917, whilst Britain was at war with the remnant of the Ottoman Empire and after Britain had been flooded with Jewish refugees from Eastern Europe, causing riots and demonstrations against them in the streets of London.[1] The Balfour Declaration called for a home for Jewish people in Palestine but added (and this is often overlooked) 'nothing shall be done which may prejudice the civil and religious rights of existing non-Jewish communities in Palestine'.

But why would the British minister for foreign affairs consider that he and his country had the right and interest to so blatantly interfere in the affairs of other peoples? It must be remembered that this was the apex of the period of colonialist ambitions, when Britain, France, Germany and Russia jostled for influence, when Germany courted Turkey and Russia coveted it, when Britain's foreign policy was bent on the protection of its routes to the jewel of its Empire, India.

Britain, on Turkey's entry into the Great War in 1914, occupied Egypt, which became a British protectorate. In November 1915, Britain, to win Arab support for its war against the Ottoman Turks committed, in the McMahon Agreement, to the independence of the Arab regions including Palestine under Arab rule. The Arabs considered these lands to encompass the entire Arabian Peninsula, east to Persia (Iran), north to Turkey, west to the Mediterranean and the border with Egypt.

Henry McMahon was the then British High Commissioner in Egypt. His dealings were with the elderly Emir Hussein.

It was for this that Lawrence of Arabia, Faisal, and the Arabs fought. Kitchener had promised: 'If the Arab nation assists England in this war England will guarantee that no intervention takes place in Arabia and will give Arabs every assistance against external foreign aggression.' The secret Sykes-Picot treaty within a year (indeed within months) was to be the first betrayal. The treaty was negotiated by British and French diplomats, respectively Sir Mark Sykes and Francois Georges-Picot, with the Russian Tsarist government as a minor party.

Pursuant to this Anglo–French–Russian accord of 1916, France got Lebanon and Syria, and Britain got Palestine, Transjordan, and Iraq and carved out Kuwait. Russia was to receive areas in Armenia and northern Anatolia but, of course, the 1917 revolution intervened. Indeed, it was the Bolsheviks who found a copy of the still-secret Sykes-Picot Agreement in the Tsarist government papers and publicised it.

Captain T.E. Lawrence commenced his legendary participation with the Arab Revolt in October 1916 when he travelled by camel from Rabegh on the Red Sea to Emir Hussein's third son Faisal's camp in the desert. It did not end until General Allenby's, and Faisal's, entry into Damascus in October 1918, shortly prior to the European armistice on 11 November.

Lawrence in the meantime had to live with his knowledge of the

Sykes-Picot treaty and its betrayal of the Arabs. Scott Anderson in his comprehensive work *Lawrence in Arabia*[2] describes Lawrence as one of 'many who regarded that policy as utterly shameful, an affront to British dignity'.

The Arab Revolt was singular by reason of the constraints placed upon it by its Arab participants. Any assistance from Allied Christian nations – Britain and France – had to be minimal. Material and logistic support – weapons and training – was accepted. Anything more, particularly European participation, was unwelcome. It aroused fears – to prove fully justified – of a later European takeover.

As World War I bogged down in Western Europe, Britain became desperate to bring the US into the conflict. This enabled Zionists to play a winning card. Zionist leaders in the US would push America to enter the war on the side of the British, if the British promised to support a Jewish home in Palestine afterwards.[3] Thus, to repeat what was said in the last chapter, from the time of the Crimean War, Palestine 'has remained at the centre of the world stage'.

When Russia, in 1917, ceased to be an effective ally, the defeat of Turkey became a more important British interest than ever. And so it was that the capture of Jerusalem by General Allenby, operating from Egypt, took on particular significance for Britain. Allenby's entry into Jerusalem, accompanied by Lawrence, was described by Lawrence as for him, 'the supreme moment of the war'.

The prospect of a friendly Zionist entity in Palestine as a buffer state for the protection of Egypt was attractive. The more so as Jewish immigrants, British Jewish immigrants, being at the same stage of political development as the British themselves, would govern themselves, thereby placing few demands on the British taxpayer, but holding out the prospect of a self-governing Dominion to the benefit of the British Empire.

Another, albeit lesser factor, has been noted. English Puritanism from John Bunyan's *The Pilgrim's Progress* (1678) to George Eliot's

Daniel Deronda (1876) set the scene for Christian Zionism. Several British ministers, brought up in the spirit of 19th century Bible-reading Protestantism, were attracted by the romantic idea of helping the Jewish people to 'return' to their promised land after 2000 years. Lloyd-George was a Welsh Baptist schoolmaster's son. In this respect they are the forerunners of late 20th and early 21st century evangelical Christians in the United States who have such a disproportionate influence on the US Presidency and Congress today.

Not everyone in the Lloyd-George Cabinet agreed. Lord Curzon asked (as well he might), 'What is to become of the people of the country?' But those under the influence of Dr Weizmann prevailed.

Although today we are astonished at this British arrogance that was so dismissive of the interests of the indigenous Arabs, there is one matter that, ironically, the British could point to in their defence. To this point of time in the history of their relations, the Jews and the Arabs had usually been friendly, and there had been no particular antagonisms between Judaism and Islam, as there had been between both Christianity and Judaism and Christianity and Islam.

And so the fate of the great-grandchildren of the indigenous inhabitants of Palestine was sealed. No more than that – great power politics – long since irrelevant, but not for the descendants.

The Balfour Declaration was of course internally inconsistent. It was not possible for there to be a 'home' as contemplated and for that 'home' not to prejudice the non-Jewish communities. This was eventually acknowledged by a British Royal Commission in 1937.[4] It was in any event apparent from the fact that for two-and-a-half years the policy of the Balfour Declaration was not published in the Middle East. This is understandable when the British promise to promote the Arab Revolt (against the Turks) is recalled. The Arabs, not surprisingly, believed the British betrayed them.

A Commission of Enquiry, set up in 1921 to enquire into the Arab riots of that year, took evidence from Dr Eder on behalf of the Zionist Commission. He claimed that, in accordance with the Balfour Declaration, Jews should be the majority of people in Palestine. It is worth noting that a British census of 1918 gave an estimate of 700,000 Arabs and 56,000 Jews. This 90 to 95 per cent of the people might be forgiven for resenting the Balfour Declaration: for being referred to as 'the existing non-Jewish communities in Palestine'. The Israelis like to point to 1949 and say, 'The Arabs wouldn't contemplate our having a State' – one might well ask, 'Why would they?'

When we consider today, nearly 100 years after the event, the significance of the Balfour Declaration, it is remarkable that British political leaders of the era could have been so insensitive to the national aspirations of the indigenous peoples. That they were is readily reflected in the work of one Herbert Sidebotham, an English commentator, whose book *England and Palestine* was published by Constable in 1918 and presented the case for a Jewish state in Palestine. It is a work of some 250 pages. It considers all of the objections to the British support of a Jewish state. Not one objection deals with the possible reaction of the indigenous population – an indigenous population approaching three-quarters of a million. Indeed, in the whole book only one sentence directly addresses the issue:

> As for the non-Jewish races in Palestine, their interests will be the special care of the protecting Power or Powers; nor is there any reason to fear that the Jews would wish to repeat the errors of the past. (*Whatever they are, and they are not elaborated upon.*)

This, it is the writer's submission, is evidence of a deep-seated British racism towards the Arabs, an attitude that they were singularly inferior, which enabled Britain and the Zionists to simply ignore their interests. The same British attitudes to the ruled, as opposed to ruling, peoples, is well described in George Orwell's *Burmese Days*, a 1930s portrayal of the dying days of British colonial society in Burma. This is much the same attitude as the Israelis display towards the Arabs today.

The only allowance that Sidebotham makes towards the Arabs is that 'the member of the Executive Council who is responsible for (the protection of the non-Jewish races) should be a non-Jew'. The fallacy and injustice of Sidebotham's thesis of the day is further demonstrated by two other extracts. When dealing with religious issues he notes that:

> the great bulk of the population in Palestine to-day is Arabian and Mohammedan. The Arab tends to feel towards the Jewish restoration in Palestine much as the Anglo-Saxon and Norman elements in England would feel to a proposal to restore the Welsh to their ancient primacy in Britain.

Finally, he asserts that the new Jewish state 'will be a force that makes for peace in the World [sic]'.

As a victorious power Britain was given Palestine as a mandated territory by the League of Nations in 1922. Indeed, the League endorsed the Balfour Declaration.

Supporters of Israel like to tell us that there was no Palestine. It was simply a part of Syria, or Jordan, or both. To the contrary, Palestine is referred to throughout history, by Herodotus in the 5th century BCE in his Histories, by Constantine in the 4th century CE in his correspondence, and throughout the times of the Arab Caliphate. In 1603 Shakespeare writes in Othello:

> Emilia: I know a lady in Venice would have walked barefoot to Palestine for a touch of his nether lip.
> *Act IV, Scene iii*

In 1863 The Religious Tract Society of London published its *Pictorial Journey Through the Holy Land; or Scenes of Palestine*. In this work Beersheba is described as the southern limit of Palestine. Beersheba lies south-east of Gaza on the northern edge of the Negev desert. Palestine is described as 'south of Lebanon'. There is no suggestion that Palestine extended east of the Jordan River.

In 1896 Herzl recognised Palestine within the Ottoman Empire: 'If His Majesty the Sultan were to give us Palestine, we

PICTORIAL JOURNEY

THROUGH THE

H O L Y   L A N D;

OR,

Scenes in Palestine.

LONDON:
THE RELIGIOUS TRACT SOCIETY;
56, PATERNOSTER ROW; 65, ST. PAUL'S CHURCHYARD; AND 164, PICCADILLY.
1862.

could in return undertake to regulate the whole finances of Turkey.'
During WW I, Australia spoke of its 'Palestine campaign'.

The fact is that, in the early years of the twentieth century,
Palestine was a widely accepted geographical entity. That the
Balfour Declaration referred to it as such is proof enough of this.
For Christians, Muslims and Jews throughout the world it had a
very real and special meaning.

At this time, the early 1920s, despite the Zionist efforts,
the percentage of the Jewish population of Palestine had not
dramatically increased. It stood at around 10 per cent. Despite the
intent of the British government and the Zionists, it remained at
about 10 per cent as late as 1933. No one, in 1917, or 1922, could
have foretold the rise and triumph of Nazism, and its dramatic
effect on the influx of Jewish peoples into Palestine.

It is the tragedy of the Palestinians that at a time when President Wilson was advocating self-determination of subject peoples following the Great War, Britain felt that it was its role to provide an answer to the 'Jewish problem'; an answer very much to the 'prejudice (of) the civil and religious rights of existing non-Jewish communities in Palestine' (Balfour Declaration). Wilson included 'the consent of the governed' among the 'Four Ends' of peace, to be embodied in the League of Nations Covenant.

Balfour himself noted the contradiction in a memorandum to the Peace Treaty at Versailles:

> The contradiction between the letter of the Covenant and the policy of the Allies is even more flagrant in the case of the independent [*sic*] nation of Palestine than in that of the independent nation of Syria. For in Palestine we do not propose even to go through the form of consulting the present inhabitants ... The four great powers are committed to Zionism and Zionism, be it right or wrong, good or bad, is rooted in age long tradition, in present needs, in future hopes, of far profounder import than the desires and prejudices of the 700,000 Arabs who now inhabit that ancient land.

Peter Mansfield in his book *The Arabs* (1978) notes:

> It is scarcely necessary to go any further than this to find justification for the Arab's sense of betrayal by the West and their special bitterness over Palestine. If the West has a feeling today that the Arabs are taking their revenge it should be easy to understand the reasons.

The 12th of Wilson's Fourteen Points asserted that the nationalities of the Ottoman Empire freed from Turkish rule 'should be assured an undoubted security of life and an absolutely unmolested opportunity of autonomous development'. In Palestine we know that they were not but it is illuminating to consider what happened to the balance of the Arabian part of the Ottoman Empire.

The Sykes-Picot treaty was effectively endorsed by the Paris Peace Conference in 1919. Syria, including Lebanon, was given to France; Palestine, Transjordan and Iraq to Britain. This was the carving up of the Ottoman Empire. Of course Egypt was already Britain's protectorate. No one wanted the obligations of colonising the poorest parts of the Arabian Peninsula – the Persian Gulf sheikdoms and Yemen – so that these backward and impoverished people were considered appropriate for independence. It was not until the 1940s and 1950s that oil was discovered on the southern shores of the Persian Gulf, in the sheikdoms and Saudi Arabia prompting one Western wag years later to comment: 'Why is our oil under their sand?'

What happened to the other 'countries'? Egypt took its independence in 1922; Saudi Arabia in 1926; Iraq in 1931. The French, of course, were not in the habit of granting independence (witness Vietnam and Algeria). However even Lebanon and Syria in 1936 gained sufficient independence to control their immigration policies; full independence was taken during WW II. Transjordan became an independent amirate in 1920 but retained a British subsidy and advisers. In 1928 it achieved modified independence sufficient to control immigration policy.

The indigenous people of Palestine, however, were not considered fit for independence or to have control over immigration before 1948. At any time before the end of WW II independence for Palestine would have meant an Arab immigration minister. An immigration minister, as John Howard and Philip Ruddock made very clear to Australians in the early years of this century, is a most important minister, because every sovereign nation has the right to say who is admitted and when.

It is ironic that the parts of the Arab world which achieved independence following the break up of the Ottoman Empire were the most socially, culturally, and economically backward, while the more sophisticated areas, including Palestine, were placed under the control of Western Christian nations.

The Paris Peace Conference had surely set the stage for the tragedy of the 20th century – recurring wars, religious schism, and brutal dictatorships – and its ramifications are with us today.

As well as looking forward from the Peace Conference, which brought World War I – the Great War – to an end, it is also interesting to look back. What was it all about? Nothing of lasting strategic importance derived from the Western Front. The only momentous changes occurred in the East – in Russia, Austria, Turkey, particularly with the Armenian dislocation, and in the Middle East – Iran, Iraq, Syria – but most of all – in Palestine.

CHAPTER 4

Resistance to Nakba

The Palestinian Arabs provided bitter resistance from as early as 1921, even when immigration was relatively small. The Palestinian National Congress, an unelected body, rejected the Mandate as long as it incorporated the Balfour Declaration. The British did not assist by appointing Sir Herbert Samuel,[1] Jew and Zionist, as High Commissioner.

By 1928 Jews amounted to 16 per cent of Palestine's population. But calls continued to be made for increased Jewish immigration as a prelude to a Jewish state in Palestine. Riots broke out in 1929, resulting in deaths of both Arabs and Jews in significant numbers.

After 1933 Arab alarm turned to despair, as large numbers of Jews coming into the country bought up the land and utilised it *to the exclusion* of all Arabs. The Arabs may well have accepted and absorbed significant Jewish immigration but for one totally inadmissible premise that underlay the whole Zionist enterprise. The Jews not only intended to introduce an alien culture, they planned to make it the only one in the country: culturally, politically, economically and demographically.[2] They insisted on Hebrew, separate schools and hospitals, self-segregation, and the exclusion of Arabs from every institution they established.

A 1938 conference called by Franklin Roosevelt at Evian in France to find a solution for Jews suffering from Hitler's terror resulted in the US, Canada and Australia offering to take a few thousand. The conference was a failure, which added to Arab bitterness. They, the Arabs, were in no way responsible for events in Europe. The evidence is clear that the reason why FDR's 1938 efforts came to nothing was because of Zionist opposition. Unless Jews were going to Palestine they, the Zionists, didn't want them going anywhere. Morris Ernst, FDR's international envoy for refugees, wrote in his memoir that when he worked to find refuge for those fleeing Hitler:

> active Jewish leaders decried, sneered and then attacked me as if I were a traitor. At one dinner party I was openly accused of furthering this plan of freer immigration (into the US) in order to undermine political Zionism.[3]

The writer might be criticised if he did not mention at this point the Grand Mufti of Jerusalem. The position of Mufti of Jerusalem was no more than that of advisor to the local governor (at this time the British through its mandate) on Muslim law. Amin al Husseini succeeded his brother Kamel as the Grand Mufti in 1921. Amin was bitterly opposed to Jewish immigration and intentions. He played a prominent role in the Arab Revolt against the British in 1936–1939, leading to his escape to Syria in 1937 – escape from possible incarceration.

The Mufti remained at large throughout the Second World War and openly supported Nazi Germany against the British position in the Middle East. There is no evidence, however, that Amin's views translated into material support for Nazi Germany from the Palestinian people. His only significant achievement was to go to Sarajevo to assist in the formation of volunteer Muslim SS battalions in the Balkans.[4]

In 1939, when the Jewish percentage of the total population was approaching one-third, Britain purported to stop further Jewish immigration. After the receipt of the MacDonald White paper, Britain asserted that it was 'not part of their policy that Palestine should become a Jewish state, that 75,000 Jewish immigrants should be admitted over the next five years, but no more after that without the approval of the Arabs'. This decision remained in force until after World War II. The revelations of the Holocaust, however, made it difficult for Britain to stop immigration both officially and via the Zionist underground. In August 1945, President Truman endorsed the Zionist demand that 100,000 Jews should be allowed immediately into Palestine.[5] The US itself took a handful – only 5000 in the two years following the War.

By 1946 a terror campaign was being waged by Jewish extremists, particularly the Stern Gang and Irgun. This campaign peaked with the blowing up of the King David Hotel in Jerusalem, the headquarters of the British administration. Ninety-one were killed, including Britons, Jews and Arabs.

By the eve of the creation of Israel, the Zionist immigration and buyout project had increased the Jewish population of Palestine to 33 per cent and land ownership from 1 per cent to approximately 6 per cent. By late 1947 the official UN estimates for Palestine were 1.3 million Arabs and 600,000 Jews. The British at last announced they would end their control of Palestine and turn the territory's fate over to the UN. Since a founding principle of the UN was self-determination of peoples, one would have expected the UN to support fair democratic elections in which inhabitants could create their own independent country. Instead, Zionists pushed for a General Assembly resolution to give them a disproportionate 55 per cent of Palestine. While they rarely announced this publicly, their stated plan was to later take the rest of Palestine.[6]

On the other side, the Arab Higher Committee issued a statement in September 1947 which advocated freedom and independence for an Arab state in the whole of Palestine which would respect human rights, fundamental freedoms and equality of all persons before the law, and would protect the legitimate rights and interests of all minorities whilst guaranteeing freedom of worship and access to the Holy Places.[7]

In 1947 the United Nations voted 33:13 (with 10 abstentions) to partition Palestine. This was at a time when the sympathy of the world lay with the Jewish people – but the West had closed its doors to Jewish refugees. The 33 chose to give another people's land (some 54 per cent of it) to the Jewish people. The Arab votes were against. Palestine itself had no vote and its views were ignored. An Arab proposal to ask the International Court of Justice to judge the competence of the General Assembly to partition a country against the wishes of a majority of its inhabitants was only narrowly defeated.

It is hardly necessary to point out that no such resolution could conceivably be passed today, or even ten years after 1947, after the addition of many Afro-Asian countries to the General Assembly.

The plan was premised on the erroneous assumption that the Arabs would simply acquiesce to having their land taken from them and voluntarily surrender majority rights, including their right to self-determination.

It should be added that of the 33 who voted in favour many went against their better judgment but were overborne by diplomatic violence and arm-twisting by the Truman White House.[8] A war-devastated France was told it would lose US aid if it voted against partition. Liberia, an impoverished African state, was told that American investment in the country would not proceed unless it voted yes. Latin American delegates were told that the proposed Pan-American highway construction project would be more likely if they voted yes. The Philippines changed its vote after intense pressure and after its delegate initially spoke against the plan.[9]

Truman himself had ignored State Department advice in supporting the Zionist plan. Truman's political adviser, Clark Clifford, believed that the Jewish vote and contributions were essential to winning the upcoming Presidential election, in which the Zionist financier Abraham Feinberg played a critical role in financing Truman's victory. He was actually credited by Truman with his presidential win.[10]

In order to strive for balance, the writer is bound to say that many Jewish peoples, expelled from Nazi Germany and its satellite states, could hardly be blamed for seeking a life in Palestine. For most, particularly after Zionist intervention, it was the only option. Nor should we forget that some 850,000 Sephardic Jews who had lived in Arab countries before 1948 largely ended up in Israel.

Having said that, there is convincing evidence that Zionists prompted Jews in Arab countries to move to Israel. Iraqi Jews had no desire to adopt Zionism. Former CIA agent Wilbur Eveland asserts it was necessary for Zionists to attack Iraqi Jews to induce them to 'flee' to Israel, and that they planted bombs in Iraqi synagogues and in an American building in an attempt to portray the Iraqis as anti-American and to terrorise the Jews.[11]

Nor should we be sceptical of such assertions. In 1948, Zionist agents were prepared to assassinate Count Folke Bernadotte, the UN representative, to undermine his peace efforts. The Stern Gang claimed responsibility for this assassination.[12] They were also prepared to embrace mass murder: witness Deir Yassin, on the night of 9 April 1948, when two-thirds of the inhabitants of this Arab village in the Jerusalem area (some 254 people) were murdered by a joint Irgun and Stern operation, carried out with the collaboration of the Haganah and the official Jewish leadership.[13]

The wrong that was done here is twofold. The Jewish communities that thrived for centuries in Morocco, Tunisia, Baghdad, Damascus, Istanbul and Seville, to mention but a few sites, should be encouraged to restore themselves.

⊰⊱

It is appropriate to consider the legal position in a little more detail. In 1947 the General Assembly of the United Nations did not authorise the creation of the State of Israel by resolution 181 (II). That resolution contemplated two States with an economic union and a United Nations administration of Jerusalem. Neither the Security Council nor the United Kingdom (the mandatory power) accepted resolution 181 (II). Jewish leaders intervened unilaterally on 14 May 1948 and declared the State of Israel. The war that followed saw further territorial gains for Israel and the resulting State bore little resemblance to that contemplated by resolution 181 (II). The Armistice Agreements of 1949 saw Israel acquire 78 per cent of historical Palestine. Premature recognition by the United States one day after the declaration, and by the Soviet Union two days after that, completed the irregular creation of the Israeli State. On 11 May 1949 Israel was admitted to the United Nations with the United Kingdom abstaining from voting.

It has been argued that the State of Israel was 'illegally recognised and improperly admitted to the United Nations'.[14]

⊗

It is of interest to note the views of prominent Australians at the time.

Australia of course voted for partition. However Australia had two quite senior officials in the UN Secretariat. The most senior was Sir Raphael Cilento[15] who served in the UN Secretariat from 1946 to 1951.

Cilento was a country South Australian boy, a scholarship student at Prince Alfred College, and a graduate from the Medical School at the University of Adelaide. He was involved with public health programmes in New Guinea, with the Australian administration that superseded the German administration following WW I. After WW II he worked with the UN in Germany and the Balkans. He became Director for Refugees and Displaced Persons from 1946 to 1947, and from 1948 was in charge of disaster relief in Palestine. He resigned in 1950 after taking the part of the Palestine refugees and returned to Australia in 1951.

The most senior Australian official in the Secretariat after him was Sir Walter Crocker, who became Australia's High Commissioner for India in 1951 and later, for many years, the lieutenant-governor of South Australia. Crocker delivered a paper on Cilento in 1984 entitled 'The Role of Sir Raphael Cilento at the UN'. In 1948 Cilento was Director of Relief Projects based in Beirut, a post that had him heavily involved with Palestine. He had actually been with Count Bernadotte a few hours before his assassination by Jewish terrorists, which prevented him reporting to the General Assembly on his attempts at establishing a successful truce.

In this paper Crocker records his own perceptions of the creation of Israel:

At the seat of the UN at Lake Success, day after day, week after week, month after month, the public galleries, the lobbies, the corridors, the cafeteria, were filled with Zionists and other Jewish zealots, pushing and persistent.

Not a few were fanatical, not a few were arrogant, all were increasingly self-confident. They were given over to the dream of turning Palestine into Israel. Their dedication was admirable.

But, unfortunately, the fact that Arabs already were inhabiting Palestine, and had done so for centuries, had no relevance for the zealots. The Arabs had no rights: they were to be torn up from their land to make way for the Jews. Their self-centredness on this point was absolute and it was not admirable.

What the Zionists later referred to as 'the miracle of Lake Success' could indeed scarcely have happened except in that place and at that time. In the name of internationalism a form of extreme nationalism was carried to victory, and in the name of the rights of small nations to independence, and of another George Washington-like war against British imperialism under another King George, a minority in Palestine, the Jews, took by force of arms the home of the indigenous majority, the Arabs.

Crocker records Cilento's belief that the creation of Israel and the manner of its creation made wounds that were unlikely to heal and, further, that the Palestinian Arabs were condemned to degradation if not genocide. Cilento was charged with anti-Semitism and, like others, his career at the UN ceased. Moreover, despite his incredible career till then, following his return to Australia in 1951 (aged only 58), he never held another official post. But, as Crocker records, to charge Cilento with anti-Semitism was 'as unfair to Cilento as was charging all Jews with the values of the Zionists or the terrorists (Jewish) of those days'. What Cilento questioned was Zionist imperialism and in that he was joined by the Vatican, by left-wing papers like the *Guardian*, and by the great majority of those who knew what was really happening.

In November 1947, at the time of the vote on partition, a vigorous debate ensued in Australia over the advisability of a Jewish state in Palestine. One person who totally opposed the plan was Australia's most eminent Jew – Sir Isaac Isaacs. Isaacs was Australia's first Australian-born governor-general (1931–1936). He was a member of the first Federal Parliament (1901–1906), a member of the High Court (1906–1930) and Chief Justice (1930–1931). He died in February 1948, two months before the creation of Israel.

In the years prior to his death he engaged in a most public debate over the advisability of that event. He opposed it and political Zionism strongly. The Zionist champion was Professor Julius Stone, a distinguished legal academic, also Jewish.

It is of interest to note the primary planks of the argument of both and consider whether 65 years of history has vindicated either. Isaacs's position was that to establish a Jewish state in Palestine would deny equal rights of citizenship to Arabs and would antagonise the Arab population in Palestine and the whole Arab world. Further, it would imperil the security of the holy places of other faiths, and it was a negation of democracy and an attempt to revert to the church-state of bygone ages. Isaacs claimed that to speak of a Jewish nationality and to regard Palestine as 'home' was to state a doctrine that might be taken from *Mein Kampf*. He asserted that a Jewish state was unwarranted by the Balfour Declaration and the Mandate and contrary to Zionist assurances given to both the Arabs and Britain.

As regards unrestricted immigration, Isaac's position was that such was a discriminatory and an undemocratic camouflage for a Jewish state. Finally, Isaacs argued that it created dual loyalty of Jewish persons to the states in which they were citizens and to a proposed Jewish state.

Stone argued that there was no danger that in a Jewish Palestine the rights of non-Jews would be prejudiced; it had been Zionist policy to assure equal rights of citizenship to non-Jews; there were no problems associated with dual loyalty; and the opening of Palestine to large-scale Jewish migration furnished the only real hope of salvation for substantial numbers of surviving European Jews.

There can be little argument that history has borne out Isaacs's fears. It could be argued that there have not been major problems with dual loyalty, and surviving European Jews were indeed desperate for somewhere to go. And whilst Isaacs's fears for the Holy Places might not yet have been justified, and his comparison with Nazi doctrines may have been emotive and unwarranted, his major arguments have all been verified by history – the rights of non-Jews have been totally compromised, those who were able to remain in Israel/Palestine are not equal citizens, and the whole of the Arab world has been more than antagonised. There are powerful, if not irrefutable, arguments that it has brought us the rise of militant Islam.

In parenthesis, on the issue of dual loyalty, we are noting the emergence of problems of some significance, with Jewish Australian citizens allegedly making their passport identities available to Mossad, and individual cases such as that of Citizen (or Prisoner) X's alleged suicide in an Israeli prison in 2010. Citizen X, one Ben Zygier, from a respected Melbourne Jewish family, had served in the Israeli military. In 2013 his family negotiated a settlement of $1.2 million from the Israeli government, with a denial of liability over his death by Israel. We shall come to the case of US-born Jonathan Pollard.

Something else should be said of dual loyalty. No doubt many Jewish people would be offended by the suggestion, particularly because one of the original charges against them was that because they were inherently nomadic, they felt they owed nothing to the state. This was one of the allegations made by the anti-Semitic press in late 19th-century France.[16]

Three prominent Australians have been mentioned. Mention should be made of three prominent citizens of the world. Albert Einstein was a German Jew. He immigrated to America in 1933 and became a US citizen in 1940. Einstein's opposition to Israel was widely known and reported on during his life. Einstein was nevertheless offered the presidency of Israel in 1952 after the death of the first president, Chaim Weizmann. Einstein declined. Whilst sympathetic to the Zionist cause, he repeatedly warned that a 'narrow nationalism' may arise if a Jewish-only state was founded and peaceful co-existence with the Palestinians was not achieved. Instead, Einstein advocated cultural Zionism – the creation of Jewish cultural and educational centres within a bi-national state with equal rights for both Arabs and Jews.[17] Einstein died in 1955.

Leon Trotsky was a Russian, or, more specifically, a Ukrainian Jew. In the years immediately prior to his assassination in 1940, Trotsky pondered upon the Jewish problem. He abandoned his hopes for assimilation in favour of a 'territorial solution'. However he did not believe that this could be Palestine and he rejected Zionism as the answer.[18]

Mahatma Gandhi was the English-trained South African lawyer who led his native Indian people to independence. In November 1938 he expressed his views on the Arab–Jew question in Palestine. He commenced by declaring his sympathies with the Jews, many of whom he had known intimately in South Africa. He asserts:

> The cry for the national home for the Jews does not make much appeal to me. Palestine belongs to the Arabs in the same sense that England belongs to the English or France to the French. It is wrong and inhuman to impose the Jews on the Arabs. What is going on in Palestine today cannot be justified by any moral code of conduct. The mandates have no sanction but that of the last war. Surely it would be a crime against humanity to reduce the proud Arabs so that Palestine can be restored to the Jews partly or wholly as their national home. The nobler course would be to insist on a just treatment of the Jews wherever they are born and bred. The Jews born in France are French in precisely the same sense that Christians born in France are French.

Gandhi then makes some observations as to what was then happening to Jews in Germany. He proceeds:

> and now a word to the Jews in Palestine. I have no doubt that they are going about it in the wrong way. The Palestine of the Biblical

conception is not a geographical tract. It is in their hearts. But if they must look to the Palestine of geography as their home, it is wrong to enter it under the shadow of the British gun. A religious act cannot be performed with the aid of the bayonet or the bomb. They can settle in Palestine only by the goodwill of the Arabs. They should seek to convert the Arab heart. There are hundreds of ways of reasoning with the Arabs, if they will only discard the help of the British bayonet. As it is, they are co-sharers with the British in despoiling a people who have done no wrong to them.

CHAPTER 5

1948 to 1967 and the
pre-1967 US/Israeli Relationship

In 1948, on the withdrawal of British forces from Palestine, the Palestinian peoples, along with their Arab neighbours, resisted what they saw, not surprisingly – or unreasonably – as the theft of their country. In the war that resulted, Israel occupied some 80 per cent of the land (26 per cent more than allocated to it by the UN). The Israelis occupied over 500 Arab villages and towns and destroyed some 380, so that the inhabitants could not return.

The late Tanya Reinhart's 2003 book *Israel/Palestine* addresses the issue.[1] An Israeli scholar and journalist, Tanya Reinhart left Israel for New York a few years before her death in 2010. She delivered the 2006 Edward Said Memorial Lecture in Adelaide, South Australia. In *Israel/Palestine* she writes:

> During the war of 1948, more than half of the Palestinian population at the time – 1,380,000 – were driven off their homeland by the Israeli Army. Though Israel officially claimed that a majority of the refugees fled and were not expelled, it still refused to allow them to return, as a UN resolution demanded shortly after the 1948 war. Thus the Israeli land was obtained through ethnic cleansing of the indigenous Palestinian inhabitants. (*The reference is to UN Res. 194*)

The fate of Palestinian refugees was addressed in UN Resolution 194, which followed the Report of Count Folke Bernadotte of 16 September 1948 recommending the right of Arab refugees to return to their homes in Jewish controlled territory at the earliest possible date. He was assassinated by Jewish terrorists on 17 September 1948 and the resolution was adopted by the General Assembly on 11 December 1948.

The Palestine War and the harsh injustices that it caused the indigenous inhabitants left a legacy of bitterness among all the Arabs against Israel and the two Western powers most responsible for its creation – Britain and the US. It has been the single most powerful factor behind the bitterness of the Arab and ultimately Muslim worlds and the growth of anti-Western feeling over the past six decades.

It is the parent of 9/11, Afghanistan, Iraq, Bali (Paddy's Pub, 2002), London (7 July 2005), the present troubles in Syria, the present troubles in Egypt, Libya, Saudi Arabia, Yemen, Bahrain, Pakistan, Somalia, et cetera. This is a far-reaching claim, and one for which the writer must answer. It is of course anathema to Zionist interests, intent on making Israel a small target. It is however clearly capable of being advanced.

Britain's responsibility has been severely but not unfairly judged by the historian Arnold Toynbee, writing in 1969:

> If Palestine had remained under Ottoman Turkish rule, or if it had become an independent Arab state in 1918, Jewish immigrants would never have been admitted into Palestine in large enough numbers to enable them to overwhelm the Palestinian Arabs in this Arab people's own country. The reason why the State of Israel exists today and why over 1,500,000 Palestinian Arabs are refugees is that, for thirty years, Jewish immigration was imposed on the Palestinian Arabs by British military power until the immigrants were sufficiently numerous and sufficiently well-armed to be able to fend for themselves with tanks and planes of their own.

In 1950 the Israeli Knesset passed the Law of Return that 'every Jew has the right to immigrate to Israel'. No such right was afforded, however, to the true, that is, the original inhabitants who now resided in refugee camps in Gaza, the West Bank, Lebanon, Syria and Egypt.

In its early years Israel was never interested in making peace with its neighbours and its so-called 'retaliatory' policies were really brutal and aggressive forms of expansionism that led, deliberately, to another war. Hence we have the 1956 and the 1967 wars. In 1956 Nasser nationalised the Suez Canal. This was the pretext for Israel, with the secret backing of Britain and France, to invade the Sinai and progress to the Canal. Once there, Britain and France sent in troops supposedly to secure the Canal for international shipping. The US, perhaps more concerned about British and French rather than Israeli activity, reacted. Eisenhower secured the withdrawal of Britain and France and, reluctantly, six months later, of Israel from Egyptian territory.

After Suez, 11 years of 'peace' ensued. Israel was supported by France, Germany and increasingly, the US. The impact of the Cold War saw the West's growing support of Israel as the USSR courted Arab governments. The year 1959 saw the establishment of the nationalist organisation, Fatah, by Palestinian exiles. In 1964 the Palestine Liberation Organization (PLO) was established with support from the Egyptian government of President Nasser. In the meantime, however, pro-Western governments in Lebanon and Jordan were 'saved' from nationalist revolutions by the West.

Ariel Sharon admits that the 1967 war had been planned by Israel two years before. The need was to expand, particularly into Syria, to secure a source of water. The same need to expel Arabs arose as in 1948. In 1967 the Israel Defense Forces (IDF) drove 80,000 Syrians from the Golan Heights. When they attempted to return to their homes, often unarmed, some were shot on sight.[2]

The 1967 war saw Israel occupy the remaining 20 per cent of Palestine. It has held it, despite UN Resolution 242, for approaching 50 years, and there should be no illusions that Israel has any intention of giving it back. Resolution 242 of 22 November 1967 was a unanimous resolution of the Security Council. It called for the withdrawal of Israeli forces from territories occupied in the war and the acknowledgment of the sovereignty, territorial integrity and political independence of every state in the area.

Following the '67 war the Israeli Cabinet set about attempting to find ways to remove Arabs from the lands occupied. A secret transfer project based on financial incentives and facilities was initiated – primarily to prompt refugees to go to Jordan. When this failed the Military Governor of the Gaza Strip, Mordechai Gur, pushed people to leave by eroding their standard of living through stopping new sources of income for refugees living in the camps. Anyone who did leave was, of course, not allowed to return.[3]

That this has been policy thereafter cannot be doubted: consider Gaza today; consider the West Bank today. We shall engage in such consideration in chapters 10 and 11.

Before leaving the pre-1967 history, let us consider the US/Israeli relationship that has contributed to Israeli belligerent militarism in no small way. The US Jewish community was a major source of funding for the Zionists from the time of the Balfour Declaration. In 1898 the first annual conference of American Zionists convened in New York. By 1922 there were 200,000 Zionists in the US and by 1948 this had grown to almost a million. Early prominent Zionists were Louis Brandeis and Felix Frankfurter – both to become prominent Supreme Court justices.

Many of Israel's pilots during the war of 1948 were Americans. President Truman played a critical role in the birth of the State of Israel through pressuring Britain to accept more refugees, supporting the UN partition plan, and arranging critical loans. After hostilities commenced, the US delegation at the UN repeatedly took Israel's side in armistice line disputes and lobbied for UN membership for Israel. This can be attributed as much to pressure from the US Jewish community, particularly through the Democratic Party, as to altruistic concern for Jews arising from the holocaust. Truman was elected in 1948 on a Democratic Party platform committed to Israel.

In the war of 1948 the US appeared to turn a blind eye to US citizens (former servicemen) fighting in the Israeli terrorist groups Haganah and Irgun. Whilst the export of arms from the US to the warring parties was illegal, the Haganah and Irgun operated quite openly in the US and gunrunning was prolific. Americans regarded the assistance of European Jewry as a humanitarian act. US tax laws were amended to provide for tax-deductible status for contributions made to the United Jewish Appeal and other Zionist organisations raising funds for Israel.

Despite the fact that Eisenhower attempted to reign in an Israel bent on expansion (thus his response to the 1956 adventure), historians generally accept that, in the years since Eisenhower, US Middle East policy has largely been determined by Israel and the US Israeli lobby. Even before the end of the Eisenhower administration, the US became a major arms supplier of Israel, enabling it to maintain a position of military superiority over all of the Arab nations combined.

Let us consider for a moment an issue that extends over a period both before and after 1967. Despite the US's publicly expressed concerns over what was happening at Dimona (Israel's nuclear facility in the Negev), the evidence suggests that the US was in fact the silent partner of Israel in that country's development of nuclear weapons. Mordechai Vanunu was the whistleblower to Israel's nuclear programme in 1986. The story of Israel's acquisition of nuclear weapons, and the preparedness of the West to turn a blind eye, contrasts dramatically with Iran's story today. The US appears to have facilitated the sale of yellowcake to Israel in the early 1960s. Neither the Johnson nor Nixon administrations acted to expose or stop the programme, rather they joined in the conspiracy of silence. France's role should not however be discounted. French engineers appear to have virtually turned Dimona into a French village in the 1960s. France appears to have all but provided the nuclear reactor.[4]

In the Six Day War of 1967 the US rendered invaluable assistance to Israel in four major ways: first, by the provision of arms in the weeks immediately preceding the war; second, by sending the 6th Fleet into the eastern Mediterranean when the Russians threatened to intervene to aid Syria after Nasser had accepted a UN ceasefire (on Syria's behalf) but which had not deterred Israel from a full-scale invasion of Syria for territorial purposes; third, by resisting any Security Council resolution for a ceasefire until Israel had achieved its objectives. Perhaps most significant was the fact that US Air Force pilots, and their planes, (with US markings painted over and replaced with Israel's) were brought to Israel the day before the war started to provide state-of-the-art military reconnaissance assistance to Israel in the war.[5] This is the 'smoking gun' evidence of co-belligerency. The US was in fact the silent partner of Israel in the 1967 war.

It should be added that it was not a 'respected' silent partner. The incident of the USS *Liberty* stands as evidence of both the arrogance of the Israeli government, and the surprising submissiveness of the American government. As the eastern Mediterranean took on the aura of a war zone in May and June 1967 the *Liberty*, a state-of-the-art spy ship, was ordered to proceed outside Egyptian territorial waters towards Israel. The *Liberty* arrived in what was by then a full-scale war zone on 7 June. The Johnson administration had made it clear that it supported the territorial integrity of all nations in the area. Such a policy was anathema to Israel's territorial ambitions, in both the West Bank and Syria (Golan Heights).

As Arab countries accepted UN calls for a ceasefire, Israel resisted and proceeded on its path, which included keeping the US as much in the dark as to its activities as it could.

On 8 June, whilst 40 kilometres off the coast of Gaza, the *Liberty*, a clearly marked United States ship in international waters, was attacked by Israeli jets, albeit unmarked jets. Israel however was the origin of the jets – it subsequently acknowledged as much and 'apologised'. The attack also came from Israeli motor torpedo boats.

Thirty-four US sailors were killed in the attack, 171 were wounded and 90 survived without injury. Evidence by US survivors was to the effect that the Israeli forces sought to kill all the ship's complement, no doubt to suggest the attack as having come from Egyptian quarters.

The *Liberty* affair was hushed up by the US government and remains to this day a source of anger and amazement to the families and friends of the dead and survivors. That Israel got away with this brazen attack on the forces of an ally says much of the power of the Jewish lobby in the US and of the lengths to which the State of Israel will go to advance its perceived interests over any others.[6]

The US/Israeli relationship is revisited in Chapter 9. There is one interesting statistic concerning this relationship, associated with the role of the United States in the Security Council. Prior to 17 March 1970 the United States had never employed its veto power in the United Nations Security Council. On that date it was used over Southern Rhodesia.

When we return to the relationship we shall see the extent to which the United States has shielded Israel in the UN from criticism and action since 1970.

Figure 1. Benjamin Disraeli
(1804–1881) twice
Prime Minister of Britain.
[The Print Collector/Getty Images]

Figure 2. Alfred Dreyfus (c. 1859–
1935), the French soldier unjustly
accused of delivering documents to
a foreign government.
[Popperfoto/Getty Images]

Figure 3. Theodor Herzl (1860–1904),
founder of Zionism.

Figure 4.
Arthur Balfour (1848–1930),
British Prime Minister in
1902–1905, later Foreign
Secretary.
[George C. Beresford/Getty Images]

Figure 5.
The 'Balfour
Declaration';
Balfour's 1917
letter to Lord
Rothschild
supporting the
establishment of
Palestine, subject
to conditions.
[The British Library/
Robana via Getty
Images]

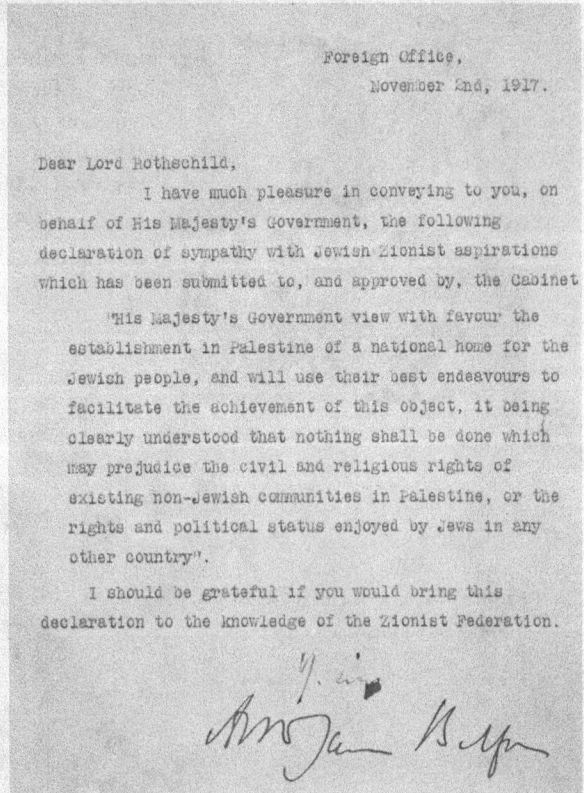

Foreign Office,
November 2nd, 1917.

Dear Lord Rothschild,

I have much pleasure in conveying to you, on
behalf of His Majesty's Government, the following
declaration of sympathy with Jewish Zionist aspirations
which has been submitted to, and approved by, the Cabinet

"His Majesty's Government view with favour the
establishment in Palestine of a national home for the
Jewish people, and will use their best endeavours to
facilitate the achievement of this object, it being
clearly understood that nothing shall be done which
may prejudice the civil and religious rights of
existing non-Jewish communities in Palestine, or the
rights and political status enjoyed by Jews in any
other country".

I should be grateful if you would bring this
declaration to the knowledge of the Zionist Federation.

Figure 6. Vera Weizmann, Dr Chaim Weizmann,
Sir Herbert Samuel, David Lloyd-George, Ethel Snowden
and Philip Snowden.

Figure 7. Sir Raphael Cilento.

Figure 8. Sir Isaac Isaacs.

Figure 9. Count Folke Bernadotte, UN Mediator, assassinated by militant Zionists in 1948.
[Kungliga biblioteket, Sweden]

Figure 10. Sir Walter Crocker, Australian diplomat.

Figure 11. Anwar Sadat, Jimmy Carter and Menachem Begin
shake hands at the signing of the 1979 Israel–Egypt Peace Treaty
at the White House.
[Library of Congress, Washington DC; photo Warren Leffler]

Figure 12. Ariel Sharon, flanked by security guards, at the Al-Aqsa Mosque,
Temple Mount, 28 September 2000. The incident provoked the
Second Intifada.
[AWAD/AFP/Getty Images]

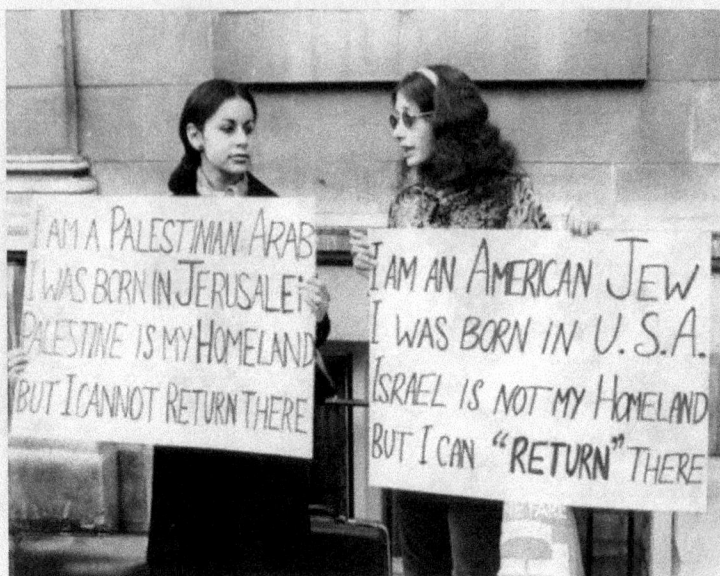

Figure 13a. Ghada Karmi and friend, protesting in the 1980s.

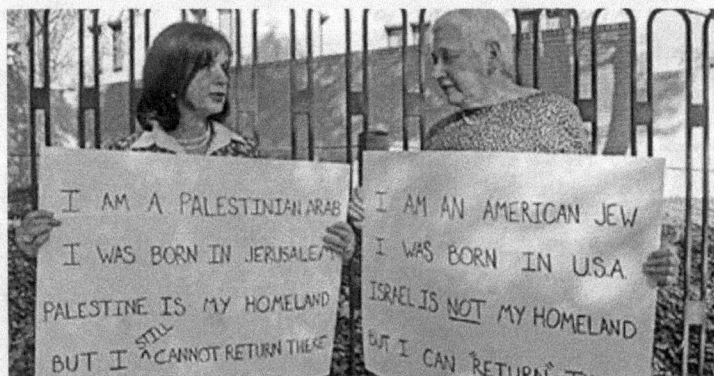

Figure 13b. Ghada Karmi and the same friend, twenty years later.

Dr Ghada Karmi is a Palestinian doctor of medicine, author and academic.
She delivered the 2007 Edward Said Memorial Lecture
in Adelaide, South Australia.

Figure 14. Prime Minister Benjamin Netanyahu speaks to the Christians United For Israel (CUFI) summit in Jerusalem, 2010.
[GALI TIBBON/AFP/Getty Images]

Figure 15. Paul Wolfowitz.

Figure 16. Martin Indyk and Shimon Peres.

Figure 17. The author's father, Sgt Delbridge Heywood Smith, (centre) at Qastina Camp, 1941.

Figure 18. Author's father (right), with colleague Sid at Port Said.

CHAPTER 6

1967 to the 21st Century

In the '67 war Israel occupied the Sinai as well as the West Bank and Gaza.

In the meantime, and commencing immediately after the 1967 war, Israel encouraged settlers to go into the Occupied Territories and take the land and build on it. How different did Israel behave from the views of some of its citizens. Amos Elon wrote in *Haaretz*, an Israeli newspaper, a week after the end of the war:

> We have a moral obligation, because the road to Israeli independence was paved on the backs of these people, and they paid, with their bodies, their property, and their future, for the pogroms in the Ukraine and the Nazi gas chambers.[1]

In 1973 Egypt and Syria sought to recover their lost territories. They joined in an all-out surprise attack on Yom Kippur, the holiest day in the Jewish year. It took some three weeks for Israel to drive the Syrians back, and to impose an inconclusive draw on Egypt. It was only able to do so with the unconditional support of the US, which had armed the Israelis. This war led ultimately to the Peace Treaty with Egypt in 1979. By this treaty, Israel withdrew from the Sinai and Egypt recognised the State of Israel. A fair reading of the treaty might suggest that Israel has not complied with it so far as its declared intentions to the Palestinians is concerned. However subsequent Egyptian governments, beholden as they have been to US aid, have not made a case against Israeli defaults.

In 1981 the Israeli government issued a fundamental policy guideline in relation to the future of the Occupied Territories:

> The (so-called) autonomy agreed at Camp David means neither sovereignty nor self-determination. The autonomy agreements

set down at Camp David are guarantees that under no conditions will a Palestinian state emerge in the territory of Western 'Eretz Yisrael'.

The reference to Camp David is to the 1978 Carter version, as opposed to the 2000 Clinton version, to which we shall come.

In 1988 an Intifada (or 'uprising') Meeting of the Palestinian National Council called for partition of historical Palestine into two independent states ... along the lines of the '67 borders, as determined by the UN Resolutions 181, 242 and 338. This is significant. Israel justified its settlement activity on the basis of a need for security given that the Arabs allegedly wanted to push Israel into the sea. Here was the white flag (and most unfortunate it was for Israel) but, not surprisingly, no peace has ensued. Israel cannot afford peace, for peace means boundaries, confinement, and the loss of the dream of a Greater Israel; the loss of its capacity to remain the only state that is a member of the UN that has no defined borders.

The Intifada was a campaign of civil disobedience and harassment of occupying forces, which lasted from the beginning of 1988 until 1992. Whilst it brought home to many Israelis the cost of continuing occupation, it took a heavy toll on the Palestinians who suffered the brunt of the associated violence and the adverse impact on the local economy.

In 1993 we arrive at the Oslo Accords, which commenced in September 1993 with a Declaration of Principles signed on the White House lawns – Oslo 1. The Palestinians re-committed to the idea of two states, involving giving up nearly 80 per cent of the historical Palestinian homeland. Israel recognised the PLO as the representative of the Palestinian people.

It is unclear what else Israel committed to other than the deferral of three topics for future negotiations – namely the question of Jerusalem, the right of return (of Palestinian refugees) and Jewish settlements in the Occupied Territories. Nothing has come of it. Oslo has been used by Israel as a cover to extend and consolidate its illegal occupation and to treble the settler population.

An Interim Israeli–Palestinian Agreement on the West Bank and Gaza, known as Oslo 2, followed in September 1995. This agreement, signed in Taba, divided the West Bank into Area A (full Palestinian control), Area B (shared civil responsibility under Israeli security control), and Area C (full Israeli civil and military control). It was also stated that 'neither side shall initiate or take any step that will change the status of the West Bank and the Gaza Strip pending the outcome of the Permanent Status negotiations'. On 4 November, Israeli Prime Minister Rabin was assassinated by an Israeli religious extremist.

The pace of implementation of the Taba Agreement was, however, extremely slow. By October 1998, 2 per cent of West Bank territory had been moved into Area A and 26 per cent into Area B, leaving 72 per cent in Area C. By March 2000, 17 per cent had been moved into Area A and 24 per cent into Area B, leaving Israel in full control of nearly 60 per cent of the West Bank. These figures have not changed since.

The attitude of the Likud government elected in 1996 was perhaps best captured by this quote from General Sharon, then foreign minister, in 1998: 'Everybody has to move, run and grab as many hilltops as they can to enlarge the settlements because everything we take now will stay ours ... Everything we don't grab will go to them.'[2]

In 2000, President Clinton, possibly seeking to restore his reputation after the Monica Lewinsky scandal prior to giving up the presidency, attempted to secure a lasting peace at the Camp David Summit.

At this summit Arafat was said to have refused a most generous 'offer', 'giving' the Palestinians some 95 per cent of the West Bank and Gaza and Jerusalem as its capital. This presentation – suggesting that the Palestinians were either ungrateful, or unrealistic, or too demanding – was put out to people around the world to encourage them to abandon any interest in the Palestinians they might have had.

It was said that all Israel wished was to annex 5–10 per cent of the land encompassing the big settlement blocs, where 150,000 Israelis already had their home. Regarding Jerusalem, Israel was prepared to divide the city and recognise part of it as the capital of the future Palestinian state. But the Palestinians wouldn't accept.

What is the truth? The truth started to come out when a US official present at the summit became too disgusted by the hypocrisy after putting up with it for a year. Robert Malley published a series of articles in the New York Times. He wrote:

> Many have come to believe that the Palestinians' rejection of Camp David exposed an underlying rejection of Israel's right to exist. But consider the facts: The Palestinians were arguing for the creation of a Palestinian state based on the … 1967 borders, living alongside Israel. They accepted the notion of Israeli annexation of West Bank territory to accommodate settlement blocs. They accepted the principle of Israeli sovereignty over the Jewish neighbourhoods of East Jerusalem – neighbourhoods that were not part of Israel before the 1967 War. And, while they insisted on recognition of the refugees' right of return, they agreed that it should be implemented in a manner that protected Israel's demographic and security interests by limiting the number of returnees.

There is in fact no documentation from Camp David. Nothing was reduced to writing because Israel would not allow it and that is why in 2013, in respect of Secretary Kerry's negotiations, the Palestinians sought transparency. Israeli prime minister, Ehud Barak, would not meet face to face with Arafat in 2000. He was afraid he might make a concession that could be held against him. All he would allow was Clinton to present US concepts to Arafat to sound them out. But in fact there never was an Israeli offer; they always stopped short. There were never any details discussed. If written down, it has been estimated the American ideas might have covered no more than a few pages.

Barak's (Clinton's) approach was based on what is known as the Beilin–Abu Mazen Plan (October 1995). According to this plan Israel would withdraw from 90–95 per cent of the Occupied

Territories; within that 5–10 per cent were 130 settlements; 50 additional settlements would remain on Palestinian land; the IDF would remain in occupation of the Jordan Valley; Palestine would recognise West Jerusalem as the capital of Israel; and Israel would recognise Al-Quds as the capital of a Palestinian state.

Quite apart from the fact that 'per se' it had nothing to recommend it, what did it actually mean?

What was intended was firstly that the 50 additional settlements would, in fact, entail 40–50 per cent of the newly created state to which Palestinians would have no access, taking into account the settlements, their land reserves and by-pass roads connecting them to Israel and each other.

The proposal that the big settlement blocs be annexed to Israel meant the land in between as well. That land was occupied by 120,000 Palestinians, but they would not become Israeli citizens since they would vote in the Palestinian elections. Thus Israel could annex the land without giving rights to Palestinian residents.

As for Jerusalem, a village by the name of Abu-Dis would actually be re-named Al-Quds – the Arab name of Jerusalem. In 1967 Israel had immediately annexed 64 square kilometres of East Jerusalem – internationally unrecognised to this day. Outside of these 64 square kilometres is the small village of Abu-Dis. By calling that Al-Quds, Israel was able to present to the World that it was dividing Jerusalem.

As for the Arab inhabitants of East Jerusalem (to become part of Israel) they would not become Israelis. Rather, Israel 'agreed' that Palestine would have the privilege of providing health, education and welfare to them; they could even have their own juridical system; but neither citizenship, nor the right to vote in Israeli elections.

Barak's unofficial map showed five isolated cantons (including Gaza) inside Israel with no external borders with any other country.

It has been estimated that had Arafat accepted these 'generous proposals' Palestine would have ended up with control over about 42 per cent of the Occupied Territories. So that, of the 90–95 per cent to form the Palestinian state, about 48 per cent is actually land to be controlled by Israel – Palestinians could not farm it or build or settle on it – even pass through it. That was the Israeli idea of sovereignty.

Clinton encouraged Arafat to come to Camp David pledging, as part of his persuasions, that he would not put the blame for a bad outcome on him. But that is precisely what, hard upon the conference's inglorious collapse, he did. And so did mainstream American, and thence, world media.

Israeli politicians often say: 'The Palestinians never miss a chance to miss a chance.' Some might think of it the other way around. Israelis never miss a chance of missing a chance. In Arafat, they had the near complete dupe. One of the reasons that the West was fooled by the fraud of Camp David was that the Palestinians were too embarrassed for the details to come out to their own people of just what they were contemplating giving away. But the Israelis lost. They could have had an honourable settlement at any time since 1988. In 20 years they have built up a well of such hatred and bitterness they will be paying for generations.

It is worth noting the Palestinian's minimum terms. In essence they have been constant since the 1974 Arab summit, which followed the 1973 war: a Palestinian state in the West Bank and Gaza; Palestinian sovereignty over East Jerusalem (including the Temple Mount but excluding the Western Wall and the Jewish Quarter); restoration of the pre-'67 border with the possibility of limited and equal exchanges of territory; evacuation of all the Israeli settlements in the Palestinian territory; and the solution of the refugee problem in agreement with Israel.

In 2002 the Arab League proffered a peace initiative. The entire Middle East agreed to officially recognise Israel if it withdrew to its pre-'67 borders allowing East Jerusalem to be the capital of a Palestinian state. Israel responded with indifference. To accept such an offer would be to give up the Zionist dream.

But let us return to September 2000: Sharon, at that time the Likud opposition leader, announced that he intended to exercise his 'elementary right' to visit 'our holy site' (Temple Mount) thereby provoking the Second Intifada. In this he received the then Prime Minister Barak's total connivance. The Israeli Army described, ominously, its war against the Palestinians at the onset of the Second Intifada as 'the second half of 1948'. It is important to note that Sharon's visit was the trigger and not the cause of the Second Intifada; the Second Intifada was inevitable, the result of years of broken promises and delays – delays designed to allow more settlement building, more appropriation, more annexation. It was to last until 2004.

In 2001 Sharon was elected as prime minister. Military rule was re-established in the Occupied Territories. The Palestinian Authority's infrastructure was destroyed. Life was made totally unbearable for the Palestinians in the hope that they will just leave. In December 2001 the Israeli Army raided the Palestinian Central Bureau of Statistics in Ramallah, destroying and confiscating computers and documents. In the words of Edward Said: 'They were effacing virtually the entire record of collective Palestinian life.' In the case of ethnic cleansing, it does not take much imagination to see how important it is to destroy records that verify that specific people actually lived in a particular place.

Operation Defensive Shield was undertaken in 2002. The Palestinian Authority was completely destroyed, thus pre-empting a Palestinian state-in-formation. The West Bank was reduced to ruins. The Palestinian Security Forces were systematically destroyed. This is important, because the Israeli government justified non-implementation of the Road Map on the basis of the Palestinian Authority not challenging the so-called 'terrorist associations'. The Road Map was George W. Bush's plan for peace in Palestine. Initiated by Bush in 2002 it was endorsed by the EU, the UN, and Russia in May 2003. Its asserted plan was an independent Palestinian state by 2005. It came to nought.

CHAPTER 7

The Wall and the
International Court of Justice

In May 2002, Israel began to erect a wall in the West Bank referring to it as a 'separation fence' or 'security barrier'. Apart from all of the other destruction that it causes, one clear purpose of the Wall (hereafter 'the wall') is the destruction of Palestinian history. Ancient buildings are bulldozed to create the wall and settler roads. The purpose is to Judaise Palestine. By targeting historical Arab sites, Israel plans to destroy Palestinian cultural heritage. Do that and they are halfway there. It is a form of cultural genocide and ethnic cleansing. It has happened particularly in Hebron and Nablus. It is in direct contravention of the Hague Convention.[1]

There is a certain attraction to the wall, because it supposedly shuts in as well as shuts out. Those who have felt for the Palestinians first asked themselves: is this something positive? Is this going to give the Palestinians respite from the creeping annexation?

But when it became apparent where the wall was being built, and how, it became clear that this was just another tool of oppression. The wall as envisaged will enclose 16.6 per cent of the West Bank, lying between it and the Green Line (the pre-'67 borders). If the Israeli government had set about building a wall on the '67 borders, rather than on occupied Palestinian land, many people would have said: 'This is good.' But if the Israeli government was prepared to do that, they wouldn't need a wall.

The sole consideration that dictates the path of the wall is the settlements, and assuring that they remain on the western side of it. But it catches Palestinian villages, leaving them on the western side of the wall as well. There is a stench associated with these villages. It is the stench of transfer. That is, transfer 'out'. For what choice do the Palestinians have, caught on the west of the wall? They cannot move. They cannot find a livelihood. Similarly other Palestinian villages are left on the east of the wall but their agricultural lands are on the west. One of the purposes of the wall, without a doubt, is to make the lives of the Palestinian inhabitants hell, in order to convince them by and by to go away, to become, with their brothers and sisters of 1948 and 1967, refugees.

But what of the International Court of Justice (ICJ)? On 8 December 2003 the UN General Assembly voted to request an Advisory Opinion from the ICJ with regard to a resolution on the legality of the construction of a security wall by Israel on the West Bank, and whether Israel was under a legal obligation to remove that wall. This was a significant development. Whilst the General Assembly has passed numerous resolutions mostly condemning the Israeli occupation in the West Bank, this was the first time the World Court had been drawn into the dispute.

The vote to request the Advisory Opinion was passed with 90 states in favour and eight opposing, namely Australia, the USA, Israel, Ethiopia, Nauru, Marshall Islands, Micronesia and Palau. Significantly, 74 states, including the European Union, abstained. The US, in opposition to the request to the ICJ, expressed the view that 'giving an advisory opinion … risks undermining the peace process and politicising the court'.

Australia took a similar position saying that the decision might 'complicate the work of the international quartet or jeopardise the implementation of the Road Map'. On the substance of the question Australia reserved its position. It urged that the lack of consent by Israel rendered the giving of an advisory opinion incompatible with the Court's judicial character; further, that an advisory opinion on the question would be 'devoid of object or purpose' and would likely have 'a detrimental effect on negotiations and on the work of the United Nations as a whole'.

Under Article 36 of its Statute, the court may give an Advisory Opinion on any legal question at the request of authorised bodies including the General Assembly. The request was:

What are the legal consequences arising from the construction of the wall being built by Israel ... as described in the report of the Secretary-General, considering the rules and principles of international law, including the Fourth Geneva Convention of 1949, and relevant Security Council and General Assembly resolutions?

On 9 July 2004, the Court handed down its Opinion, that the construction of the wall by Israel is in breach of international law and that it violates principles of the UN Charter and norms prohibiting the threat or uses of force and the acquisition of territory. The construction of the wall was also found to be inconsistent with the right of self-determination of the Palestinian people. More significantly, the Court also said that all states should not recognise 'the illegal situation resulting from the construction of the wall'. It also urged states not to give any aid or assistance in maintaining the status quo.

An Advisory Opinion is supposed to clarify the legal position on a specific matter. While, in general not legally binding, such opinions have in the past led to UN sanctions to compel conduct consistent with the normative legal position expressed in the Opinion.

In this case, in handing down its Opinion, the Court also noted that the Security Council and the General Assembly might consider taking steps to ensure compliance by Israel with the Opinion. Consistent with UN practice, the Court forwarded its Opinion to the Secretary-General, who in turn advised the General Assembly and the Security Council accordingly. Under the UN Charter, resolutions of the General Assembly are in general not legally binding, decisions of the Security Council adopted in accordance with the Charter are. It was therefore left to the Security Council to compel Israeli compliance if the Council deemed it appropriate.

In the immediate aftermath of the publication of the Opinion, Israel declared that it would seek the support of the US to veto any Security Council resolution relating to the Opinion and the wall and the US did indeed indicate that it would veto attempts by the Council to adopt a resolution on the issue. Both houses of Congress passed overwhelming resolutions deploring the ICJ ruling.

On 20 July 2004 the Tenth Emergency Session of the General Assembly resumed to consider the Opinion. It adopted Resolution GA10248 condemning Israel's construction of the wall and calling on it to dismantle the structures and abide by the Court's Opinion. The resolution was adopted by a vote of 150 states in favour. Ten abstained while Australia joined five other countries (the USA, Federated States of Micronesia, Israel, Marshall Islands and Palau) in voting against the resolution. It is noticeable that, on both occasions at the General Assembly, Australia and the US were the only two OECD states to vote against the resolutions.

It is often the case that the Western press will pass judgment on a country, be it Syria, Iran, North Korea, Zimbabwe, Venezuela, by painting it as being in conflict with the 'international community'. No doubt in some cases it will be justified in so doing. The Western press does not paint Israel and the US as being out of step with the 'international community'. Yet no clearer example of that occurring exists than as demonstrated by this particular vote.

⊰≫⊱

A significant element associated with the wall (or 'barrier' as it was referred to by the Court) is the introduction of a system of 'Closed Areas'. In early October 2003 the Israeli Defense Force issued orders declaring land that lies between the barrier and the Green Line in the north-west part of the West Bank to be 'Closed Areas'. According to the Secretary-General's report, the declaration affects '73 square kilometres and approximately 5300 Palestinians living in 15 communities'. As the report notes:

> The Orders introduce a new system of resident status. Only on issuance of a permit or ID card by IDF will residents of the Closed Area be able to remain and will others be granted access to it. Israeli citizens, Israeli permanent residents and those eligible to

immigrate to Israel in accordance with the Law of Return can remain in or move freely to, from and within the Closed Area without a similar permit.

Some years have passed since the Secretary-General's report. What has been the result of the 'permit regime'? In 2013, one Idan Landau summarised the report of the Israeli NGO HaMoked: Centre for the Defense of the Individual in an op-ed entitled 'A journey into the dark heart of Israel's permit regime'. He summarised the position:

> Trapped between the separation barrier and the Green Line, Palestinians living in the 'Seam Zone' are forced to reckon with a Kafkaesque permit regime that appears designed to do one thing and one thing only: make them give up and leave.

The 'Seam Zone' is the area between the wall and the 1967 Green Line. It expropriates (at this point in time)[2] 9.4 per cent of the territory of the West Bank. More than half of this is private Palestinian land.

Permanent residents of the villages in the Seam Zone must apply for a permit to live on their own lands – lands that have been theirs from time immemorial. To obtain a permit residents must prove that exceptional circumstances apply to them. In other words their lands are stolen from them in the all but exceptional cases. This only applies to Palestinians. Jews from Brooklyn or Melbourne do not have to establish 'exceptional circumstances'.

Thirteen categories of permit are contemplated and complexity is designed to produce a result. Permits are usually for three months only. A Palestinian's status is always temporary – regardless that they were born there and have lived there all their lives. A permit for one purpose may not be used for another. Lose one and you lose all and they are so encumbered with conditions they are easily, and intentionally, lost. The number (of Palestinians) holding permits is steadily decreasing. Renewal of permits is an administrative nightmare – resulting in reduced access to lands – lands that need to be worked. No work, no produce, no income – and the need to leave to maintain life.

In the administrative process, time limits exist at every turn – miss one and the right to a permit, even assuming the Palestinian can establish 'exceptional circumstances', is lost. The land is lost. An American Jew from Brooklyn picks it up. Applications get lost in the system. The applicant has a new onus. Appeals take six months. In the interim crops are unworked and lost. The Palestinian must live. He gets the message. He gives up. The goal of annexation is achieved.

To say that the construction of the wall and the introduction of the system of closed areas impacts adversely on the affected Palestinian communities is an understatement. Israel used to argue that the barrier is a 'legitimate temporary security measure'. Statements from many Israeli government members elected in 2013 suggest no such thing.

⚜

Significant legal issues were raised for consideration by the International Court. First, there was the question as to whether Israel is an 'occupying power' in the Territories and whether the construction of the barrier is consistent with its obligations as an occupying power. Assuming that Israel is indeed an occupying power, then the legal issue was whether the construction of the barrier is consistent with its obligations towards the Palestinians as a 'Protected People' or whether the barrier might be permissible under the Fourth Geneva Convention as a 'restrictive measure'. Secondly, there arose the question as to whether the construction of the barrier could constitute an inchoate territorial claim, with adverse implications for the settlement of the conflict. Thirdly, there was the issue of whether the barrier undermines the right of self-determination of the Palestinian people. Finally, given the prevalence of resistance activities against Israel from aggrieved Palestinians, could Israel justify the construction of the barrier as a legitimate act of self-defence?

The Court made the following findings.

First, Israel is an occupying power in the Territories including in and around East Jerusalem. The construction of the wall in the occupied territory is contrary to international law.

Second, Israel is obliged to terminate these breaches of international law; to cease construction of the wall in the occupied territory, dismantle those bits already built there, and repeal or render ineffective associated legislative and regulatory measures.

Third, Israel is obliged to pay reparation for damage caused by construction of the wall in the occupied territory, including in and around East Jerusalem.

Fourth, all states are obliged not to recognise the illegal situation resulting from the construction of the wall, nor to assist in the maintenance of that situation; furthermore all parties to the Fourth Geneva Convention relative to the Protection of Civilian Persons in Time of War 1949 (and almost all states are parties) are obliged to ensure compliance by Israel with international humanitarian law as embodied in the Convention.

Finally, the UN, especially the Security Council and the General Assembly, should consider what further action is required to bring to an end the illegal situation arising from the construction of the wall and its associated regime.

That is the decision in outline. Judge Buergenthal, from the US, was in all but one ruling, in a minority of one to 14 in favour. The 14 spoke for the 'international community'. The international community does not, on this issue, include the United States.

Within these sparse conclusions are some important legal issues.

International humanitarian law is the law concerning the conduct of armed hostilities and the protection of human rights during armed hostilities. The law is found mostly in the Geneva Conventions of 1949 on the protection of victims of armed conflicts. Of particular relevance is the Fourth Geneva Convention relative to the Protection of Civilian Persons in Time of War, 1949, to which Israel is a party. The court rejected Israel's contention that it was not obliged to apply the Fourth Geneva Convention because it only applied to occupation of territory falling under the sovereignty of a party to the Convention. According to Israel, the relevant territory occupied by it had not been under the sovereignty of a party to the Convention; hence it did not apply. The court disagreed. Because the territory had been under Jordanian control prior to Israeli occupation in 1967, the crucial element that triggered the application of that law was an outbreak of hostilities between two parties to the Fourth Convention, Israel and Jordan. This finding is important not because it says anything particularly new but rather because it sets out very clearly the basis for the application of international humanitarian law in the Occupied Territories.

The Court also addressed the right of self-determination. Here the Court considered the impact of the deliberate transfer by Israel of its nationals into the Occupied Territories as settlers. This action is in breach of Article 49(6) of the Fourth Geneva Convention, which prohibits the introduction by the occupying power of its own nationals into the occupied territory.

According to the Court, the wall could bring about a de facto annexation if it remained in place long enough. That risk, combined with other factors including the illegal establishment of Israeli settlements, severe restrictions on the lives of thousands of Palestinians living in the affected Territories, as well as the resulting departure of Palestinian populations from certain affected areas, 'severely impede the exercise by the Palestinian people of its right to self-determination'.

What is important here is the way the Court picked up the issue of population transfers and, apart from asserting the illegality of such actions per se, stressed their possible impact on the right to self-determination.

The discussion by the court of human rights law and its application in the Territories concluded with a finding that Israel is in serious breach of its obligations. The court concludes:

> The wall, along the route chosen, and its associated regime gravely infringe a number of rights of Palestinians residing in the territory occupied by Israel, and the infringements resulting from that route cannot be justified by military exigencies or by the requirements of national security or public order.

The Court's treatment of the self-defence issue is brief. Israel had asserted that the construction of the wall was consistent with its 'inherent right to self-defence'. Israel's argument was that since the right of self-defence entitled states to use force in self-defence, they must be entitled to take actions short of force in self-defence too, including non-forcible measures such as the construction of the wall. Thus Israel argued it was entitled to use territory that did not belong to it to construct a barrier to protect not only its own territory but also the lives and interests of Israeli citizens who had settled in the Occupied Territories with governmental approval, in breach of the law of occupation and the fundamental rights of the indigenous inhabitants of those Territories.

The Court found that the right of self-defence did not apply because there was no armed attack against Israel by another state. Israel's problem was building the wall in the Occupied Territories. If Israeli settlers were not located there – a situation of Israel's own making – they would not require protection. The problem was they were seeking to defend its citizens in Occupied Territories where they had no right to be.

Some have argued that an Opinion from the ICJ offers no real assistance in the search for a durable solution. But the only reason that it has not is the veto of the US. A Security Council intent on respecting the position of the Court could authorise sanctions. Whilst Israeli defiance is inevitable, without its backer it could not thumb its nose at the international community as it has.[3]

CHAPTER 8

The 2006 Lebanese War

In January 2006 two significant events occurred: Ariel Sharon, then prime minister, suffered two massive strokes leaving him incapacitated, and Hamas won elections to the Palestinian National Authority. Hamas refused to recognise Israel. The West, led by the US, refused to recognise the democratically elected Hamas government. Hamas was resisted by Fatah, which retained control of the US/Israeli funded security apparatus. The green light for an attack on Hamas by Israel could not have flashed brighter.

The immediate catalyst for the violence in 2006 was the tunnelling from Gaza by a group of Palestinians and the capture of an Israeli soldier, Gilad Shalit, and death of two others, along with the deaths of two of the Palestinian raiders. This attack was into pre-'67 Israeli territory.

After a week or so of massive retaliation by the IDF in Gaza a second group of Arab fighters, under the banner of Hezbollah, made a similar raid from Lebanon into Israel and this time captured two soldiers whilst causing the deaths of eight. Arab casualties were not reported and this action provoked a massive response by Israel. Hezbollah targets deep within Lebanon were attacked by air strikes. Hezbollah responded with rocket attacks causing in turn a full-scale ground invasion by the IDF, which met stiff and successful resistance from Hezbollah.

Many would argue that both these acts were legitimate acts of resistance against an occupation that had persisted for nearly 40 years. It is, in international law, an illegal occupation, and recognised as such by the World Community reflected in UN resolutions (181, 242, 338) and the (9.7.2004) decision of the International Court of Justice on the legality of the wall.

In fact, Israel lost the public relations war after Israeli Prime Minister Olmert made the mistake of declaring his intention to 'set Lebanon back 20 years'. Television coverage showed the Israeli devastation of Lebanon.

At first sight, George W. Bush's statement that the United States supported the right of Israel to defend itself sounds reasonable. Australia of course picked up on this argument. However, when one scratches the surface, it appears to be no more than a mantra that hides the true position. It ignores the antecedents. It does not ask why the Gazan Palestinians perpetrated their raid but invites the listener to view the situation as if, for example, out of the blue, a group of Indonesian soldiers attacked an Australian Army base in Darwin.

The reason, of course, that the Gazan Palestinians so acted is that they are players in a conflict that, at the least, goes back to 1967 when Israel occupied Palestinian land, the 22 per cent rump of historical Palestine left to them after the 1949 war. That occupation had persisted for 40 years. It is an illegal occupation.

People might ask, Well, how does that relate to Lebanon, there is no illegal occupation there? There are two answers. The first is that the illegal occupation includes that of the Golan Heights (Syrian land) and the Shebaa Farms area, claimed by Lebanon. But more importantly we are talking here of one conflict. The fighters in Hezbollah include the grandsons and daughters of Palestinian refugees, people expelled from Palestine in 1949 and forced to live in refugee camps ever since. The fight to end the occupation is their fight. The desire to come to the aid of their brothers and sisters in Gaza and the West Bank is more than a desire, it is a necessity.

And so, when Israeli government spokesmen say 'Israel has a right to defend itself', what it is really saying is: 'Israel has a right to perpetuate the illegal occupation of the West Bank, Gaza, the Golan, and the Shebaa Farms, and to attempt to steal as much land from the Palestinians as it can through the agency of its settlers, and to thereby deny the legitimate aspirations of the Palestinian people to their own sovereign state, and freedom.'

Over the preceding 40 years Israel has constructed more than 220 Jewish-only colonies, with over 500,000 Israeli settlers, on 60 per cent of occupied Palestinian territory.

Israeli supporters will retort: 'Ah, but they want to destroy the State of Israel.' True, there are Palestinians and other Arabs and Muslims who do, and there are Israeli political parties who similarly call for a Jewish state in all of the lands west of the Jordan River thus denying the right of the Palestinians to exist. Indeed, the reality of the situation is that Israel has, for almost six decades, failed to recognise the Palestinians and that is the problem.

Israeli supporters say: 'They won't accept our right to exist.' But which Israel are they asking us (the world) to accept as having a right to exist? Is it an Israel co-extensive with the lands that Israel currently controls, being all lands west of the Jordan? Is it a smaller Israel that Israel will converge to unilaterally but which will occupy 60 per cent of the West Bank, i.e. Area C?[1] Is it an Israel that includes the Golan, i.e. Syrian land? Is it an Israel that has sovereignty over Arab air space over Gaza? Which Israel is it? There is no basis in international law for any of those Israels to exist.

Any unbiased observer would agree that were Israel (and the United States) to comply with UN resolutions, end the occupation, allow a Palestinian state in the West Bank and Gaza and seek to live in harmony with that state, the best chance for peace in the Middle East will have come to fruition. The irredentists on both sides will continue to cause trouble. But the heat will have been removed for the great majority in both communities and, in time, reconciliation will occur.

Finally it must be remembered that the UN Charter provides that territorial changes imposed by force will not be recognised by UN members. Former Prime Minister Olmert once asserted that he would unilaterally re-draw the borders to include into Israel the major settlement blocks and the Jordan Valley. But under international law Israel is required to withdraw from every square inch of land it seized in June 1967.

Israel says 'There is no partner in peace'. For that read: 'There is no partner prepared to capitulate. We cannot find someone who will legitimise their own dispossession as the price of living unmolested on a few isolated patches of their ancestral land.' Since 1988 when the Palestinian National Council voted to accept a two state solution based on the 1967 borders, Israel has had such a partner if it wanted it. It didn't want it because it didn't want to give up any of the West Bank or Gaza.

We hear: 'Missiles that are being fired into Israel were made in Iran.' This is a curious argument. Where were the missiles being used to kill civilians in Lebanon and Gaza made? Have Seattle and Miami been annexed to Israel?

We hear: 'The Government of Israel has officially announced that the fence [*sic*] is a temporary means of security and does not reflect any political or other border.' And yet E-1, the land west of the wall, appeared in Olmert's convergence plan as land to be retained by Israel.

Tony Blair once said: 'The root cause of the problem is Muslim fundamentalists intent on undermining democracy in Iraq, Lebanon and the Palestine Territories.' Yet it was Blair who joined with George W. Bush in calling for non-recognition of the Hamas-led government in Gaza a day after it was lawfully and democratically elected in 2006.

There is a desperate need for a new international (*not US-led or sponsored*) diplomatic process based on international law and human rights, aimed first at ending the occupation – all of it – and establishing equal rights for all. That is the only basis for a just, lasting, comprehensive peace in the region.

In parenthesis, Hezbollah 'won' the 2006 Lebanon war. That assessment takes into account what had gone before, the victories of 1948 and 1967 in particular, and also the fact that the captured Israeli soldiers were not returned, the fact that Hezbollah was not destroyed, the fact that northern Israeli cities were hit and damaged by rocket attacks, and the fact that Israeli casualties were real. Shalit was not released by Hamas until a prisoner exchange in October 2011.

Israel was generally blamed for the conflict – for use of disproportionate force. The Arab world was euphoric. Nasrullah (Hezbollah's leader) was a hero. Arab heads were held high.

CHAPTER 9

The US/Israeli Relationship – Part 2

No attempt is made to record the entire history from 1967 to now concerning US–Israeli relations: the massive assistance given by Nixon in 1973 to turn a potential defeat of Israel into a half victory, the support of the militarists, and the blind subservience to Israeli policy. No better instance of this was the rewarding of Israel for non-participation in the first Gulf War (1991). Israel received debt cancellation and massive military aid. The biggest item, however, was a US $10 billion loan to provide housing for Soviet Jews settling in Palestine. This loan was initially held up but finally released during the heat of the 1992 Presidential elections.

The US since 1967 has resisted all attempts at international engagement, presenting itself as the sole peacemaker when in fact it has been a co-belligerent. By shielding Israel from international scrutiny, the US has enabled Israel to consolidate its occupation of Palestinian and other Arab territories.

Let us return to the use of the US veto in the Security Council as one of its five permanent members. There are an additional ten non-permanent members. Between 10 September 1972 and 2013 the US used the veto 42 times. It is worth considering a few (12) of the votes. In each instance the 'one (1)' is the United States:

- 26 July 1973 – (The Motion) affirmed the rights of the Palestinian people to self-determination, statehood and equal protections. Vote: 13 – 1, with China absent.
- 25 March 1976 – (The Motion) deplored Israel's altering of the status of Jerusalem, which is recognised as an international city by most world nations and the United Nations. Vote: 14 – 1.

- 20 January 1982 – (The Motion) demanded Israel's withdrawal from the Golan Heights. Vote: 9 – 1, with 4 abstentions.

- 20 April 1982 – (The Motion) condemned an Israeli soldier who shot 11 Muslim worshippers on the Temple Mount ... near the Al-Aqsa Mosque. Vote: 14 – 1.

- 8 June 1982 – (The Motion) urged sanctions against Israel if it did not withdraw from its invasion of Lebanon. Vote: 14 – 1.

- 2 August 1983 – (The Motion) condemned continued Israeli settlements in occupied Palestine territories of West Bank and Gaza Strip, denouncing them as an obstacle to peace. Vote: 13 – 1, with 1 abstention.

- 6 September 1984 – (the Motion) deplored Israel's brutal massacre of Arabs in Lebanon and urged its withdrawal. Vote: 14 – 1.

- 31 May 1990 – (The Motion) called for a fact-finding mission on abuses against Palestinians in Israeli-occupied lands. Vote: 14 – 1.

- 17 May 1995 – (The Motion) declared invalid Israel's expropriation of land in East Jerusalem in violation of Security Council resolutions and the Fourth Geneva Convention. Vote: 14 – 1.

- 7 March 1997 – (The Motion) called on Israel to refrain from settlement activity and all other actions in the Occupied Territories. Vote: 14 – 1.

- 26 March 2001 – (The Motion) called for the deployment of a UN observer force in the West Bank and Gaza. Vote: 9 – 1, with 4 abstentions.

- 14 October 2003 – (The Motion) raised concerns about Israel's building of a security fence through the occupied West Bank. Vote: 10 – 1, with 4 abstentions.

As is apparent again, whatever its meaning, the phrase 'international community' does not include the United States.

But in addition to the veto, the US of course has the view that there are Security Council resolutions (presumably 'core') and then there are other Security Council resolutions (presumably 'not core'). In June and August 1980 the Security Council declared Israel's annexation of Jerusalem 'null and void' under international law. In December 1981, the Security Council similarly declared Israel's annexation of the Golan Heights 'null and void'.

On 9 August 1990 the Security Council declared Iraq's annexation of Kuwait 'null and void' under international law. For this last declaration only, however, would the West insist on the strict application of international law and create its 'Coalition of the Willing'. Arabs could be forgiven for thinking there was one rule of law for Israelis and another for non-Israelis. Thus we see the US vetoing the 20 January 1982 Motion demanding withdrawal from the Golan Heights.

It is appropriate to reflect on the fact that many of the votes just recorded were 14–1. That means that Britain and France voted in favour of the motion. The US was prepared to stand alone – to stand alone against the rest of the world as represented by the other four permanent members and the ten non-permanent members of the day. The US is the so-called promoter of democracy, the proponent of the majority view. On this issue however there would be no compromise. There are apparently limits to democracy.

When looking for reasons for US partiality it is not difficult to find them. Israel started, understandably, with the sympathy of the world, courtesy of fascism. Israel thereafter was skilful in painting itself as the underdog, when it was never that. It was able to present itself as an outpost of the West, a potential friend in a sea of darkness. This was the time of the Cold War. There were also logistical factors in its favour. American Jews have been steadfast in their support of Israel, aware that, without US support, Israel would be in real danger of imploding.

Jewish tax-exempt groups, benefitting massively from the US federal government and many state and local governments, by way in particular of tax-deductible donations, are estimated to give upward of two billion dollars per annum to Israel.[1]

American Jews have striven to hold political sway in the US. Mitchell Bard[2] in an article entitled 'The Israeli and Arab Lobbies' writes:

> This is reflected by the fact that Jews have the highest percentage voter turnout of any ethnic group. Though the Jewish population in the United States is roughly six million (about 2.3% of the total US population), roughly 89 per cent live in twelve key electoral college states. These states alone are worth enough electoral votes to elect the president. If you add the non-Jews shown by opinion polls to be as pro-Israel as Jews, it is clear Israel has the support of one of the largest veto groups in the country.
>
> The political activism of Jews forces congressmen with presidential ambitions to consider what a mixed voting record on Israel-related issues may mean in their political future. There are no benefits to candidates taking an openly anti-Israel stance and considerable costs in both loss of campaign contributions and votes from Jews and non-Jews alike. Potential candidates therefore have an incentive to be pro-Israel; this reinforces support for Israel in Congress. Actual candidates must be particularly sensitive to the concerns of Jewish voters: it follows that the successful candidate's foreign policy will be influenced, although not bound, by the promises that had to be made during the campaign.

By contrast, there are only approximately 1.2 million Arabs in the US including only about 70,000 Palestinians. This Arab population is concentrated in five states: California, Florida, Michigan, New Jersey and New York – all key to the electoral college, but in all (save Michigan) the Arab population is dwarfed by that of Jews.

Jews have occupied positions of influence in consecutive US governments. The Clinton administration had several Jewish Cabinet members and, remarkably, for a country trying to at least sell itself as an honest broker, had as its principal Mideast negotiator, an American Jew (Dennis Ross). Ross of course re-emerged in Obama's administration; as did Martin Indyk in July of 2013 as the US special envoy in the latest round of negotiations. Indyk is anything but a neutral participant. His strong and unmistakable pro-Israel credentials are unquestioned.

In the George W. Bush administration the neo-conservative brain trust was almost exclusively Jewish, with practising Jews, Paul Wolfowitz and Richard Perle in particular positions of power. Not only did Bush pander to the Jewish–American vote by agreeing with Sharon, he also pandered to his fundamentalist Christian base. About 30 per cent of the American population is evangelical Christian, with roughly three-quarters of those who might be called hard-core fundamentalists.

American evangelism is not new to Palestine and particularly Jerusalem. The passionate Protestantism of America saw Warder Cressor appointed as the first US Consul General of Syria and Jerusalem in 1844. Montefiore notes that 'he had been a Shaker, a Millerite, a Mormon and a Campbellite before a local rabbi in Pennsylvania convinced him that salvation was of the Jews whose return would bring the Second Coming'.

Now what, you may ask, is the significance of that for the Arab–Israeli conflict? There are many references in the Old Testament, here is one:

> Thus saith the Lord God: Behold, I will take the children of Israel from among the nations, whither they be gone, and will gather them on every side, and bring them into their own land.[3]

Some so-called Evangelicals, particularly the dominionist and theocratic elements,[4] believe that the creation of the State of Israel is fulfilment of biblical prophecy. Only when the Jews have been gathered to Israel and the Third Temple built, will Jesus return to Earth. Jesus's return will give rise to the last days and the Rapture in which Christians are taken up to heaven.

And where will the Third Temple be built – why, of course, where the Second Temple is supposed to have been – on Temple Mount, site of the Al-Aqsa Mosque and the third holiest shrine of Islam. For some fundamentalists, Jewish and Christian – often educated people – the Temple has become the great cargo ship. For the settlers, the Temple Mount has become a rallying call. Their potential to aggravate conflict between Jew and Arab for their purposes is the spot that symbolises the dispute between Jew and Arab – Temple Mount.

Gorenberg, in his book *End of Days*, points out that US fundamentalist Christians (Christian Zionists) regard the peace process as the work of the Antichrist. Christian Zionist churches in the US have given millions to settlement projects in the Occupied Territories. The late Jerry Falwell and Pat Robertson, both prominent evangelicals, were and are well-known advocates of Christian Zionism. Falwell describes the creation of the State of Israel as the most important event in human history since Christ's ascension and is:

> ... proof that the second coming of Jesus Christ is nigh ... Without a State of Israel in the Holy land, there can not be the second coming of Jesus Christ, nor can there be a Last Judgment, nor the End of the World.[5]

Netanyahu, during his first prime ministership, 'courted evangelicals as allies against the Clinton administration and its efforts to push ahead with the peace process'. Gorenberg notes:

> The Netanyahu–evangelical alliance reached its most public display when Netanyahu came to Washington in January 1998 to discuss Israel's stalled withdrawal from parts of the West Bank under the Oslo Accords. Before sitting down with Clinton, Netanyahu was feted at a rally organised by Voices United for Israel, a group bringing together conservative Christians and Jews, where the crowd greeted him with a chant of 'not one inch!' and speakers included Reverend Jerry Falwell.[6]

Netanyahu was subsequently a member of Sharon's Cabinet and then again the prime minister.

Fundamentalist Christians were in Bush's White House from top to bottom. It is these people who demanded war in Iraq and then broadened their horizons to Iran and Syria. It is these same people who encouraged the Likud Party to jettison Oslo and the concept of giving up land for peace.

The Rev. Dr Stephen Sizer is an Anglican and Chairman of the International Bible Society in the UK. In Christian Zionism; Justifying Apartheid in the Name of God he claims that Christian Zionism has become the most powerful and destructive force at work in America today, shaping foreign policy on the Middle East and inciting hatred between Jews and Muslims.

What is said in chapters 2 and 3 is repeated: 'from the time of the Crimean War Palestine has remained at the centre of the world stage.'

❦

And what of Barack Obama? In his Cairo speech in June 2009, Obama declared 'two states for two peoples' and demanded that Israel halt further settlements while negotiations proceeded. He was soon obliged to back down.

In September 2010 the Obama administration brought together President Abbas and Prime Minister Netanyahu for their first face-to-face meeting in two years, after Netanyahu agreed to a ten-month settlement freeze at the beginning of the year. When the freeze expired shortly after the talks began the negotiations ceased. Israel refused to renew the moratorium on construction in the settlements claiming it would only do so if the Palestinians would recognise Israel as a 'Jewish state'.

In July 2013 the second Obama administration appointed Martin Indyk 'special envoy to *shepherd* (Israeli/Palestinian) talks toward a final settlement'. (Emphasis added.)

Indyk began working in 1982 as a deputy research director for the American Israel Public Affairs Committee (AIPAC), the most powerful pro-Israel lobbying group in the US Congress. He was a co-founder of the AIPAC-linked Washington Institute for Near East Policy and readily acknowledges his Jewish identity and commitment to Israel. He is a board member of the New Israel

Fund and of the National Security Studies in Israel and a member of the advisory board of the Israel Democracy Institute. Professor Lawrence Davidson of West Chester University, Pennsylvania, has described him as:

> an outright Zionist whose lack of impartiality contributed to the failure of peace talks under the Clinton administration. There is no secret about this, nor is there any apparent embarrassment on the part of the Obama administration at simultaneously claiming to be a worthwhile mediator while assigning an overtly prejudiced envoy to the talks.[7]

The negotiations will of course ignore international law, and instead we will have the pro-Israel arbiter determining and declaring the Israeli positions and its 'painful compromises' to be 'reasonable'. In the meantime Israel will continue to build and expand settlements. If the Palestinians reject any 'reasonable' proposals the US will label them as having blocked peace.

Professor Davidson continues:

> The only conclusion that can be drawn from this is that, if there is a 'settlement', it will be a pro-Israeli one forced upon a Palestinian National Authority which, in any case, is made up of people who are not representative of the Palestinians at large and really have no legal standing to negotiate anything, much less a final status agreement. Is this a formula for future peace? Of course not; but it is what the Zionist lobby finds acceptable.[8]

Richard Falk, the UN Special Rapporteur for Palestinian Territories, has mused in respect of Indyk's appointment, 'perhaps there was no viable alternative; Israel would not come even to negotiate negotiations without being reassured in advance by an Indyk-like appointment. And if Israel had signalled its disapproval, Washington would have been paralysed'.

We have seen the disclosures of Edward Snowden in mid-2013. Remarkably, through Snowden, we learn that the US National Security Agency shares raw intelligence data with Israel without first removing information about US citizens. Pursuant to a memorandum of understanding, the US government hands over intercepted communications likely to contain phone calls and emails of American citizens. The agreement imposes no restraints on the use of the data by Israel.[9] What is even more surprising is that this agreement was signed only two months after Barack Obama assumed office. This reflects a subservience of the US to Israel that unfortunately Americans unthinkingly accept. We have Edward Snowden to thank for the fact that Americans might start thinking about it.

Compare this revelation with the case of Jonathan Pollard. Pollard, an American Jew (dual loyalty (above)), passed classified information to Israel while working as an American civilian intelligence analyst. He was convicted and sentenced by the US to life imprisonment in 1987. Israel granted Pollard citizenship in 1995, despite the obvious fact that he was not a resident. In 2002 Pollard was visited in prison by Benjamin Netanyahu. There have been high-profile attempts to secure his release. Apart from the Israeli government, prominent US citizens such as Henry Kissinger, Newt Gingrich and Dan Quayle have made public calls to President Obama to commute his sentence. Pollard is eligible for parole on 21 November 2015.

Clearly, the United States is today more captive to Israel than it was in 1985 when Pollard was arrested and charged. And it is the more so whenever elections are coming up and candidates need campaign funding – funding that AIPAC helps provide thanks to the 2010 US Supreme Court decision allowing political action committees (PACs). Super PACs enable Zionist organisations to purchase members of Congress without the public knowing. Because the funds do not go directly to candidates, the amount of money spent does not have to be declared.

At time of writing Senator Barbara Boxer is spearheading the US–Israel Strategic Partnership Act, backed by AIPAC, which legislates for the inclusion of Israel in the US visa-waiver programme, thereby allowing Israelis to enter the US without a visa.

It is appropriate to reflect on what is an American Jew. What is a secular American Jew? Twenty-two per cent of American Jews now describe themselves as having no religion. That figure rises to 32 per cent for those born after 1980.[10] Is this secular American Jew an American? Is he/she a Jew? Is he or she an Israeli living in the US? Why do Jewish American organisations regard assimilation as the greatest danger? Religious Jews no doubt have a reason to call themselves Jews. But non-religious American Jews no longer suffer discrimination – they are no longer denied access to the local country (golf) club, or, more importantly, business or civic institutions. Why can't they just be American? The answer is – Israel.

Is there however a light at the end of the tunnel? Professor Lawrence Davidson[11] refers to a piece by M.J. Rosenberg entitled 'Will AIPAC Defeat Obama on Iran?' and notes Rosenberg's observation that, ultimately, it is money that suborns Congress.

> Why, he asks, would any in Congress pass measures that go against the interests of their own country and risk involvement in yet another Middle Eastern war? 'The answer is simply that the midterm elections are coming up and that means members of Congress need campaign cash. And AIPAC provides it.' Fortunately, there is a catch to this rather corrupt process. The alliance between politicians and the Zionist lobby depends on a passive citizenry that does not threaten electoral defeat of politicians who promote special interest wars when the voters want peace. Right now, the voters do not seem very passive.

CHAPTER 10

Today

And so we arrive at today. The position of the Palestinian is seemingly hopeless. He watches (as he has done for over 60 years) and sees the Israelis come onto his land and build a settlement. The settlers either uproot the olive trees that he tended with his father and grandfather as a child, or confiscate them for themselves. This is easily done by simply saying that the trees are a security risk – snipers could hide in them.

He has no job, he lives in poverty. He watches the bulldozer come in and bulldoze his house. If he resists, the Israeli government screams 'terrorist' but, more painful than that, the US and the world's media call him a terrorist. By so labelling him, Israel and the West systematically suppress the reality of the Palestinian experience of dispossession and make it possible to ignore the Palestinians' undeniable claims to the land. The Palestinian is in despair; he has been rendered peripheral; he is isolated; his sense is only of displacement and loss. He probably feels how a Jew in 1930s Germany felt.

In Gaza, prior to the unilateral evacuation of settlers in 2005, some 7000 Israeli settlers with military appurtenances and bypass roads occupied about a third of the land. The total area of that land is only 365 square kilometres. Somehow, in the remaining two thirds, 1.3 million Palestinians survived. Following the evacuation of settlers those Palestinians were sealed from the outside world and live in a ghetto whose total economy is controlled by the Israelis. Their living standards are appalling. They have been largely forgotten by the world – by the John Howards, Kevin Rudds, Julia Gillards and Tony Abbotts of this world who say 'I am totally committed to Israel' – worse – 'Australia is totally committed to Israel' – or, worse again: 'Australia supports the right of Israel to exist.' Israel's right to exist has not been and is not in question.

People may think, well, here's a positive development, Sharon removed the settlers from Gaza. But the *quid pro quo* was the creation of more West Bank settlements. And when Palestinians had the misfortune to elect a Hamas government – quite democratically – Israel saw the necessity to punish them by imposing a stranglehold on Gaza, its access to the world, its economy, its life. After the overthrow of the Morsi government in Egypt in 2013, Israel has a collaborator in the Egyptian military government, cutting off the lifelines from Gaza to Egypt.

The position is much the same in the West Bank. In January 2004 Gideon Levy, a highly respected Israeli journalist, described a recent visit to Nablus. He wrote:

> One sees Nablus declining relentlessly into its death throes. This is not a village that's dying behind the concrete obstacles and earth ramparts that cut it off from the world; this is a city with an ancient history, which until just recently was a vibrant, bustling metropolis that boasted an intense commercial life ... a captivating urban landscape and age-old objects of beauty.
>
> An hour's drive from Tel Aviv, a great Palestinian city is dying, and another of the occupation's goals is being realised. It's not only that the splendid homes have been laid waste, not only that such a large number of the city's residents, many of them innocent, have been killed; the entire society is flickering and will soon be extinguished. A similar fate has visited Jenin, Qalqilyah, Tul Karm and Bethlehem, but in Nablus the impact of the death throes is more powerful because of the city's importance as a district capital and because of its beauty ... But the true wound lies far deeper than the physical destruction: an economic, cultural and social fabric that is disintegrating and a generation that has known only a life of emptiness and despair. More than any other place in the territories, a state of anarchy is palpably close here.

We have to this point only spoken of the West Bank; not of Jerusalem. The wall surrounds occupied East Jerusalem and is merely another step in the long-term strategy of confiscating as much Palestinian land as possible, whilst simultaneously encouraging the Palestinian population to leave. As with the wall in the rest of the Occupied Territories, the wall in Jerusalem is being built well within Palestinian Territory. The effect is that Jerusalem is totally separated from the remainder of the Occupied West Bank.

In the Old City there are four quarters: Jewish, Christian, Armenian and Muslim. They are named such for a reason. It is because, for hundreds of years, the predominant if not exclusive occupation of the particular quarter has been by the ethnic and religious group giving the quarter its name.

There is no need for a change to this. The UN when voting for partition in 1947 proposed that the Old City would be an internationally protected area. Consider the position today. Jews are now buying up Arab properties, often by deception through intermediary third parties, aiming to 'reclaim' the ancient Muslim Quarter. Israeli security guards obstruct access by Palestinians to their homes, encouraging them to leave.

The Judaisation of the Old City ought not to be acceptable to the world. There is no reason for it. Jewish organisations funded by wealthy American Jews are funding settler activities in East Jerusalem.[1]

∻

Let us consider the settlers in the Occupied Territories (not just East Jerusalem) in a little more detail. The Israeli government has consistently provided tax breaks to settlers to move into the Occupied Territories.

In fact the settlements are heavily subsidised by the Israeli government. It's an attractive proposition if you are an upper-middle class Israeli. You get very cheap housing in a newly constructed upscale neighbourhood – exclusive of Arabs, since regional councils approve who can move in.

Settler violence often occurs with the tacit consent of the IDF and perpetrators are rarely punished. The Israeli authorities' failure to protect Palestinians from such acts of violence violates its obligations under Article 27 of the Fourth Geneva Convention.

The Israeli government speaks of 'natural growth'. But natural growth applies only to Jews. Under Oslo 2, 60 per cent of the West Bank is Area C – under full Israeli control. In Area C, schools, kindergartens and water are only for Jews. In Area C the settlers have unlimited water; but Palestinians have a quota (of their own water) not adequate for human needs.[2]

Figures for the United Nations Relief and Works Agency, known as UNRWA, note that in March 2011, 76 Palestinian homes or structures in the Occupied Territories were demolished and 158 people were forcibly displaced, including 64 children. UNRWA asserts that this has a devastating impact, particularly on women and children whose lives are destroyed along with their homes. At the same time, the number of Jewish homes being built in contravention of international law on Palestinian land is rising to record highs. The UN High Commissioner for Human Rights has condemned this discrimination.

The occupation has always been about settlement, *not* security, since Israel could have militarily occupied the West Bank and Gaza in 1967 indefinitely without establishing a single settlement, and could withdraw from all its settlements tomorrow and maintain military occupation until it felt secure enough to turn the territory over to Palestinians.[3]

Human Rights Watch (HRW) published a 166-page report in December 2010 that compared Israel's treatment of Israelis and Palestinians in Area C. Its conclusion: Israel lavishes money on the settlements, their infrastructure, and their quality of life, while spending next to nothing on Palestinians. Worse, there seems to be a deliberate policy of weakening the Palestinian sector, while controlling its lands, resources and, in general, making life difficult for Palestinians.

Israeli policies have led to the consistent and rapid expansion of settlements in the Occupied Territories, the population of which grew from approximately 240,000 inhabitants in 1992 to roughly 490,000 in 2010, including East Jerusalem. While Israeli policymakers are fighting for the 'natural growth' of their illegal settlements, they're strangling historic Palestinian communities, forbidding families from expanding their homes by denying planning approval, and making life unbearable.

A Palestinian community that HRW examines is Jubbet al-Dhib, a village with 160 residents south-east of Bethlehem that dates from 1929. The village's only connection to a paved road is a rough 1.5 kilometre dirt track. Children must walk to schools in other villages several kilometres away because their village has no school.

Israeli authorities have refused requests to connect Jubbet al-Dhib to the Israeli electric grid, and also rejected an international donor-funded project that would have provided the village with solar-powered streetlights. Any meat or milk in the village must be eaten the same day due to lack of refrigeration. Villagers depend on candles for light, or kerosene lanterns.

Approximately 350 metres away is the Jewish community of Sde Bar, founded in 1997. It has paved access roads for its population of 50 and is connected to Jerusalem by a new highway, which bypasses Palestinian cities, towns and villages. Sde Bar operates a high school, closed to students from Jubbet al-Dhib. Sde Bar has all modern amenities, particularly electric lights, which Jubbet al-Dhib villagers can see from their homes at night.

Israel claims that differential treatment is justified by security needs. But no security rationale can explain the vast scale of differential treatment, such as permit denials that prohibit Palestinians from building or repairing homes, schools, roads, and water tanks, HRW asserts. The Association for Civil Rights in Israel has charged Israeli authorities with denying permits to Palestinians to build on and develop their lands – *their lands* – in order to allocate those lands to Jews for parking, entertainment, archaeological digs or settlement construction.

We come to Operation Cast Lead: Gaza – December 2008/January 2009. In order to justify the use of modern weapons of destruction on an all but defenceless people it was necessary to paint the Gazans as demons, ruled over by the terrorist organisation Hamas. The result was some 1400 Palestinian deaths including many children. On the Israeli side, ten soldiers and three civilians were killed. The UN's Goldstone Report of September 2009 found both sides guilty of war crimes. In discussing the report at its publication Goldstone described the respective war crimes of the two sides as quite unbalanced – Israel being guilty of far greater and more heinous crimes. Goldstone became the subject of a campaign of smear and innuendo, particularly in the US, and ultimately withdrew his name from the Report.

When the usual Zionist suspects plead with the ordinary reader 'What other country would put up with rockets into their land day after day, month after month?', one might ask: 'What other country has illegally occupied its neighbour for over 40 years?' The only reason that Israel has maintained a blockade of Gaza and hence continued its occupation, apart of course from the desire to destroy Hamas, is that if Gaza were able to conduct itself like any other sovereign nation it would arm the West Bank. That is unacceptable to Israel, which has pencilled the West Bank in for ethnic cleansing and ultimate annexation.

CHAPTER 11

Myths and Other Issues

Anti-Semitism

It is true that whenever Israel is criticised by any person who identifies as an anti-Zionist a charge of anti-Semitism is made. This does a grave injustice to concerned people all over the world who oppose what they see as Israel's racism, genocide, and ethnic cleansing directed at Palestinians.

The charges of anti-Semitism should be rejected for what they are, an attempt to deflect criticism away from Israel. The charges are designed to indicate to critics that moving beyond the boundaries within which Zionists are prepared to debate must mean that the critic is motivated by hate.

However, so far as the media is concerned, in Australia (as well, of course, in many other Western countries) Israel enjoys a remarkably good press since anti-Palestinian, or anti-Muslim bias permeates our media.

A poll in the early 2000s in Europe suggesting 53 per cent of the population considered Israel the greatest present threat to world peace is not the result of a new anti-Semitism. It is a slander on the European majority to suggest that.

There are, of course, many Israeli Jews and non-Israeli Jews who are totally opposed to the Israeli government policies. They might have a commitment to the State of Israel and that can be well understood. They are, however, hampered by the historical fact that non-Israeli Jewish communities, particularly in the United States but in the West generally, have given unqualified support to the successive (successive – since 1948) repressive governments: Labour, Kadima and Likud. They are, as well, compromised by the Law of Return, granting them, (unless they renounce it, and it does not appear to be renounceable although some have tried), the right at any time to take up citizenship in Israel, or the Occupied Territories for that matter.

Having said all that, it could not be suggested that there is no anti-Semitism in the West. Many would say that it pales into insignificance compared to racism directed at Muslims, and Arabs in particular.

ANTI-SEMITISM (NOUN): ANY CRITICISM OF ISRAEL WHATSOEVER

Racism

What is racism? Simply, a belief in the superiority of a particular race; and antagonism towards other races based on this.

Edward Said in his 1979 paper 'Zionism from the standpoint of its victims'[1] draws attention to a secret (but subsequently leaked) report by a ministry official, one Israel Koenig, to then Prime Minister Rabin. Koenig's plan discusses the social engineering required to use the Arab's backward 'Levantine character' against itself. Since Arabs in Israel are a disadvantaged community, the reality must be enhanced as follows:

> The reception criteria for Arab university students should be the same as for Jewish students and this must also apply to the granting of scholarships. A meticulous implementation of these rules will produce a natural selection and will considerably reduce

the number of Arab students. Accordingly, the number of low-standard graduates will also decrease, a fact that will facilitate their absorption in work after studies. (*Said comments: The plan here is to make certain that young Arabs would easily be assimilated into menial jobs, ensuring their intellectual emasculation.*)

Encourage the channelling of (Arab) students into technical professions, the physical and natural sciences. These studies leave less time for dabbling in nationalism and the dropout rate is higher.

Make trips abroad for studies easier while making the return and employment more difficult – this policy is apt to encourage their emigration.

These policies apply only to Israeli Arabs, not Arabs in the Occupied Territories, who of course are not allowed to study in Israel. Such policies evidence the readily recognisable benevolence towards Jews and paternal hostility toward the inferior natives, the Arabs.

Israeli racism is best demonstrated with reference to its one million Israeli Arabs – within Israel itself. Deprived of a constitution or Bill of Rights, the Israeli Arab must confront in his/her daily life the organisations having quasi-sovereign status such as the Jewish Agency and the Jewish National Fund. These organisations exist only to promote Jews and ensure, through that objective, discriminations against Palestinians of every conceivable kind. Thus Israeli Palestinians have no right to live in areas reserved by law for Jews (i.e. over 90 per cent of the country).

David Hirst, writing in *The Gun and the Olive Branch* in 2003, notes:[2]

A community representing 20 per cent of the population is confined to municipal areas amounting to 2.5 per cent of the total. While 700 Jewish settlements were established since the state came into being, not a single new town or village has been built for a Palestinian population now over six times its original number. In 1998, despite a vastly greater need, out of 429 localities classified as 'priority areas', and therefore qualifying for special budgetary assistance, only four were Palestinian. Some 70,000 Palestinians live in over 100 villages which ... the government does not 'recognise', even though most of them pre-exist the state of Israel itself. Being 'unrecognised', they appear on no map, they are denied basic services such as mains water, electricity, sanitation and paved roads; though desperately overcrowded, they are forbidden to construct new houses, or even erect a tent; since they are also forbidden to repair existing houses – let alone add an extension, a lavatory or a bathroom when these fall into disrepair, whereupon the government, ruling them unsafe, orders their demolition. That, in fact, was the objective from the outset. For the real, if unavowed, reason for their 'non-recognition' is that they and the land that comes with them are destined to join that estimated 96 per cent of formerly Palestinian-owned territory which has already passed into Jewish hands.

One piece of evidence of the racism practised by the Israeli government against the Palestinians was reported in the Guardian newspaper in January 2004. And it relates to water, a rare commodity in Palestine. Israel has three key water resources: the Sea of Galilee and two natural underground aquifers – the 'mountain aquifer' in the West Bank and the 'coastal aquifer' in Israel. Recently more reliance has been placed on the mountain aquifer in the Occupied Territories. It might be thought that the Palestinians, if not controlling this aquifer, would at least be able to share it proportionately with the Israelis. Not in the least. The Palestinians are not allowed to drill a well without Israeli approval. More than 80 per cent of water from the West Bank goes to Israel. The Palestinians are allotted just 18 per cent of the water extracted from their own land.

The *Guardian* reports:

Palestinian villages and farmers are monitored by meters fitted to pumps and punished for overuse. Jewish settlers are not so constrained, and permitted to use more advanced pumping equipment that means the settlers use 10 times as much water per capita as each Palestinian.

Ten years have passed since the *Guardian* so reported. Today, Israel sells desalinated water to the Palestinians in the Occupied Territories. There would be no need for the Palestinian Authority to buy water if it controlled its own natural water resource flowing under its lands. Amira Hass reports in *Haaretz* in February 2014 that, of the water extracted from West Bank aquifers, some 20 per cent goes to Palestinians living in the West Bank and about 80 per cent goes to Israelis on both sides of the Green Line.

∽⟨⟩∽

It is perhaps appropriate to stand back and consider the position. We have addressed the US/Israeli relationship. We have considered the impact of Christian Zionism. The next section of this chapter, Genocide and Ethnic Cleansing, will comment upon the significance of the American government shutdown in October 2013.

What is the connection? Might it possibly be Christian fundamentalism in the US South and Midwest? This is the home of Christian Zionism. What is the history of white Southerners? It is of course the history of slavery. It is the history of white supremacy. Blacks were inferior to whites. (Arabs are inferior to Jews.)

Just as white Southerners considered blacks as permanent outsiders, so too do Israeli Jews consider the Palestinian Arabs as outsiders – untrustworthy fellow citizens.

Just as the white Southerner opposed inter-racial marriage, so too does the Israeli Jew. In September 2013, the *Times* of Israel reported on a hotline that allows callers to inform on Jewish–Arab couples.[3] When called, the line announces that its service is designed to 'save the daughters of Israel'. 'If you are in contact with a goy (non-Jewish man) and need assistance, press 1.' 'If you know a girl who is involved with a goy and you want to help her, press 2.' There are other options. One is a prayer for those in need. The prayer beseeches the Almighty 'to put proper understanding in the heart of the woman', that she may go 'from darkness to light, from *slavery* to redemption' (emphasis added).

Just as the white Southerner feared black violence, so the Israeli Jew fears the Arab: the Jew is the reliable member of society – the Arab is the degenerate.

The Tea Party Republican (aka Christian Zionist) considers that no government is better than an Obama (supposedly liberal) government; the Israeli Jew who supports his government considers that no accommodation with the Arab is appropriate.

Racism in Israel is the vice that dare not speak its name. Is the country that condones such racism the 'light unto the nations' which it professes itself to be?

Yonatan Mendel, a correspondent for the Israeli news agency Walla, wrote in the *London Review of Books* in 2008.[4] He was at the time of writing at Queen's College, Cambridge, working on a PhD that studies the connection between the Arabic language and security in Israel. He writes:

> If the Israeli parliament legislates that 13 per cent of the country's lands can be sold only to Jews, then it is a racist parliament. If in 60 years the country has had only one Arab minister, then Israel has had racist governments. If in 60 years of demonstrations rubber bullets and live ammunition have been used only on Arab demonstrators, then Israel has a racist police. If 75 per cent of Israelis admit that they would refuse to have an Arab neighbour, then it is a racist society. By not acknowledging that Israel is a place where racism shapes relations between Jews and Arabs, Israeli Jews render themselves unable to deal with the problem or even with the reality of their own lives.

Genocide and Ethnic Cleansing

In his 1979 article, Edward Said notes that Theodor Herzl's diary records that the mass of poor natives were to be expropriated and:

> The property owners will come over to our side. Both the expropriation and the removal of the poor must be carried out discreetly and circumspectly ... spiriting the penniless population across the border by procuring employment for it in the transit countries, while denying it any employment in our own country.

Let the owners of immovable property believe that they are cheating us, selling us things for more than they are worth. But we are not going to sell them anything back.

Said also visits the diaries of Joseph Weitz, who from 1932 was the director of the Jewish National Land Fund. In 1965 his diaries were published in Israel. On 19 December 1940 he wrote:

It must be clear that there is no room for both peoples in this country ... the only solution is Eretz Israel, or at least Western Eretz Israel, without Arabs. There is no room for compromise on this point! ... there is no way besides transferring the Arabs from here to the neighbouring countries, to transfer them all; except maybe for Bethlehem, Nazareth and Old Jerusalem, we must not leave a single village, not a single tribe. And the transfer must be directed to Iraq, to Syria, and even to Transjordan. For that purpose we'll find money ... And only with such a transfer will the country be able to absorb millions of our brothers, and the Jewish question shall be solved, once and for all.

We know that Herzl was not of a religious bent. Today, however, the settlers and their supporters regard ethnic cleansing of the Arabs as an imperative, even a commandment from Yahweh. They cite the Book of Numbers, Chapter 33, in which the Lord is said to have spoken thus to Moses:

When you have crossed the Jordan into the land of Canaan, then you shall drive out all the inhabitants of the land before you, destroy all their engraved stones, destroy all their moulded images, and demolish all their high places; you shall dispossess the inhabitants of the land and dwell in it, for I have given you the land to possess.

We are reminded of Lucretius – 'so great is the power of religion to lead us to evil'.

Tanya Reinhart was the Israeli scholar and columnist cited in Chapter 5. She notes the statistics pertaining to Palestinian injuries – 25,000 reported to December 2001 since the start of the First Intifada. She notes the standard IDF assertion that some Palestinians were injured by 'stray bullets'. She questions how it can be that 'stray bullets' have a remarkable tendency to overwhelmingly strike eyes, the head, or knees. Tanya Reinhart makes this allegation:

> Israel's systematic policy of injuring Palestinians cannot be explained as self-defence, nor as a spontaneous reaction to terror. It is an act of ethnic cleansing – the process through which an ethnic group is driven from a land that another group wishes to control. In a place so closely observed by the world as Israel/ Palestine, ethnic cleansing cannot be a sudden act of massive slaughter and land evacuation. Rather, it is a repetitive process by which people are slowly forced to perish or flee.[5]

USA Today is a popular mainstream American media publication. In February 2002 it published an article advocating the 'transfer' of Palestinians from the Occupied Territories to Jordan. One of the current government parties is committed to such 'transfer', otherwise known as ethnic cleansing, a war crime for which Milosovic was tried in The Hague. Under the Geneva Convention it comes within the definition of genocide. It is a reflection of how far the US and its so-called 'Christian' society, together with its media, have sunk that this sort of material is published without outrage.

David Hirst is the author of *The Gun and the Olive Branch*.[6] He is a widely respected journalist who has covered the Middle East for decades. In an article entitled 'Pursuing the Millennium' on Jewish fundamentalism published in February 2004 he writes that the West is largely ignorant of Jewish fundamentalism. According to Jewish fundamentalists, he asserts:

> Force is the only way to deal with the Palestinians. So long as they stay in the Land of Israel, they can only do so as 'resident aliens' without 'equality of human and civil rights,' those being 'a foreign democratic principle' that does not apply to them. But, in the end, they must leave. There are two ways in which that can

happen. One is 'enforced emigration'. The other way is based on the biblical injunction to 'annihilate the memory of Amalek'. In an article on 'The Command of Genocide in the Bible', Rabbi Israel Hess opined – without incurring any criticism from a state Rabbinate whose official duty it is to correct error wherever it finds it – that 'the day will come when we shall all be called upon to wage this war for the annihilation of Amalek'. He advanced two reasons for this. One was the need to ensure 'racial purity'. The other lay in 'the antagonism between Israel and Amalek as an expression of the antagonism between light and darkness, the pure and the unclean.

Jewish fundamentalists are thought to account for some 20–25 per cent of the Israeli population, higher than the number of Shia Muslim fundamentalists in Iran. Jewish fundamentalists seek a 'Jewish Kingdom', governed by Jewish religious law, of which the rabbis would be the sole interpreters. The Knesset would be replaced by a Sanhedrin, or supreme judicial, ecclesiastic and administrative council. Men and women would be segregated in public, adultery would be a capital offence, and anyone who drove on the Sabbath would be liable to death by stoning. Non-Jews would have the status of 'resident aliens' and live in a state of servitude; such is the contempt which Jewish fundamentalists hold for Christians, which renders ironic the adoration that America's evangelicals have for Israel.

It is important however not to restrict such views to Israel. In late 2013 the US government was shut down consequent upon a Congressional stalemate. The instigators of the shutdown were Tea Party Republicans, the standard bearers of Christian dominionism. Not for them Obama's 'socialism' (Obamacare). For them, their 'church can be the new government'.[7]

The shutdown eventually ended. That does not mean that the Christian Right has stopped believing that Obamacare portends the end times. Some on the Christian Right believe that Obamacare might be predicated by Revelations: that is, Obamacare will require all citizens to have a microchip implanted – the 'mark of the beast' predicted in Revelations that portends the return of Christ and the end of the World.[8]

According to the Christian Right 'God wanted unregulated economic freedom (American capitalism) and minimalist government to prevail'. God also apparently wants, and the Christian Right is there to advance, the US as 'a Christian fundamentalist nation'.[9]

These are the voters who elect the government which votes against a motion in the Security Council calling on Israel to refrain from settlement activity and all other actions in the Occupied Territories: carried, 14 – 1, (7 March 1997).

And then we have the Shia and Sunni divide, and the civil war in Syria, and its impact throughout the Muslim world, particularly in Iraq, Iran, Afghanistan, Libya, Egypt, Chechnya and Chinese Turkestan. We are reminded yet again of Lucretius.

Israel is a nuclear power. We worry about Pakistan, which is not occupying and has not occupied a neighbour for over 40 years. Nor is it in rapture over a Third Temple.[10]

Jewish fundamentalists have embarked on a process of genocide; witness Baruch Goldstein's murder in 1994 of 29 Muslim worshippers in Hebron's Mosque. This act was praised by many rabbis and Goldstein was elevated to the status of martyr.

Tanya Reinhart again: as early as October 2000, immediately after Sharon's visit to the Temple Mount, she asserts that there seemed to be a well-prepared list of places in the West Bank (particularly near Jerusalem) targeted for attack, places to which Israel kept returning in ensuing months. She cites Beit Jala as such a place and writes:

> It is hard to avoid the conclusion that Israel has targeted these areas for a slow, forced evacuation that will eventually enable their annexation with the fewest possible Palestinians remaining.

She notes that the pretext for Israeli military action against this 'peaceful, middle class, cosmopolitan neighbourhood' was an alleged Palestinian shooting from Beit Jala into the neighbouring Jewish suburb of Gilo. However, she records that the Israeli press interviewed the local Tanzim commander (Tanzim being a youth militia arm of Fatah) who alleged that they caught Israeli collaborators who admitted that they fired, and that they, the Tanzim, were trying to calm the situation, not wishing to give the Israelis the opportunity to destroy Beit Jala. You may wonder who to believe in a case like that. But you are aware of the IDF's capacity to pinpoint a moving car in Gaza and destroy it with missiles. Ms Reinhart similarly muses:

> It remains a mystery how the sophisticated and well-equipped Israeli army was not able to directly hit the Palestinian snipers. Instead, it had to bombard Beit Jala every night with shells, and turn its northwest quarter into a ghost town (like) a small Sarajevo.

Ms Reinhart continues:

> During the period between October 2000 and December 2001, a clear picture emerged – beyond the countless details of daily brutality and cruelty – of a systematic Israeli effort to break Palestinian society and destroy its infrastructures. A painfully precise summary was offered by Taher Masri – a Jordanian statesman of Palestinian descent – in an interview with Newsweek in December 2001. Masri explained that Israel has been working on three levels: The first level 'is to destroy the economic infrastructure of the Palestinian territories, which are largely agricultural and, formerly, touristic. During the Israeli incursions into Bethlehem earlier this year, for instance, troops systematically trashed newly built tourist hotels'. As part of this strategy, in large areas olive and citrus trees have been cut down or bulldozed. The second level is 'to destroy the tools of the Palestinian Authority, the police and security apparatus. At the same time that Sharon demands Arafat crack down on Hamas and Islamic Jihad, Israel has in recent months destroyed 80% of the PA's police headquarters ... Thirdly, 'Sharon is eliminating – liquidating – the Palestinian

leadership. He is hitting the third rank now, but he will move up to the first. Without leadership, without economic lifeblood, without security tools for the PA, the people will be ready to leave the country'.

You will have heard the news reports from Israel. Have you ever thought it curious that everyone assassinated by Israel is described as a 'ticking bomb'? The assassination policy is part of the 'war on terror'. Israel has stood beside its friend the United States in this war – and since 9/11 literally anything goes.

Well, is all this action working? Between October 2000 and June 2001 more that 150,000 Palestinians left for Jordan. These were largely Christian Arab families from the middle class. Forcing out a society's elites is a part of the process of ethnic cleansing, and makes the remaining population that much more vulnerable.

Israel targets international aid as well. Prior to the 2006 Lebanese war, Israel banned aid in the form of food and medicine from Iran and Iraq. That was easy of course because those two countries were part of the 'Axis of Evil'. But it systematically pressures the EU to stop aid, asserting that such aid is assisting 'terrorists'. From mid 2002 Israel has targeted UNRWA, the UN Relief and Works Agency, upon whom a substantial proportion of the Palestinian population depends for the basics of life. Again, the charge is that the refugee camps, where UNRWA operates, are terrorist havens. The demand is that the UNRWA become a force in the war on terror by reporting to the Israelis on 'terrorist activity' in the refugee camps. In April 2004, UNRWA announced that Israeli constraints upon its operations made the continued provision of assistance to Gazans impossible.

Resistance

One would like to think that Palestinian resistance could be channelled into the non-violent variety that proved successful, largely, in South Africa. It is acknowledged that there was armed and violent resistance in South Africa, which paralleled the non-violent demonstrations.

However that is not to say that armed resistance is not justified. In January 2002, David Grossman, the Israeli novelist, in response to news of the seizure of a Palestinian ship attempting to smuggle arms into the Occupied Territories said this:

> What proof has been obtained here? Proof that if you oppress a people for 35 years, and humiliate its leaders, and harass its population, and do not give them a glimmer of hope, the members of this people will try to assert themselves in any way possible? And would any of us behave differently than the Palestinians have in such a situation? And did we behave any differently when for years we were under occupation and tyranny? Avshalom Feinberg and Yosef Lishansky set out for Cairo to bring money from there to the Nili underground so that the Jewish community in Palestine could assert itself against the Turks. The fighters of the Haganah, the Lehi and the Etzel underground movements collected and hid as many weapons as they could, and their splendid sliks (arms caches) are to this day a symbol of the fight for survival and the longing for liberty, as were the daring weapons acquisition missions during the British Mandate (which were defined by the British as acts of terror). When 'we' did these things, they were not terrorist in nature. They were legitimate actions of a people fighting for its life and liberty. When the Palestinians do them, they become 'proof' of everything we have been so keen to prove for years now.

This should be said, finally, on suicide bombers. Palestinian atrocities come, after all, in the service of what the world regards as a legitimate purpose, the ending of occupation. Israeli atrocities come in the service of an illegitimate purpose, the perpetuation of that occupation. Moreover it was Herzl who adopted the saying: 'He who desires the end desires the means.' As Hirst however notes:

> But in proposing such an end – a Jewish state in Palestine – and such means, he was proposing a great deception, and laying open his whole movement to the subsequent charge that in any true historical perspective the Zionists were the original aggressors

in the Middle East, the real pioneers of violence, and that Arab violence, however cruel and fanatical it might eventually become, was an inevitable reaction to theirs.[11]

The Palestinians have always rejected reasonable compromise
In 1935 the British government offered a limited measure of self-government. Though not impartial, it was much less weighted in the Zionists' favour. The Zionist Congress categorically rejected it.

On the other hand the Zionists have always welcomed 'Arab refusal'. Such refusal has always given them their excuse, i.e. no choice but to fight. If in the process they gained more than they planned or hoped for, that was their good fortune. The Arabs, they said, had only themselves to blame. An Israeli scholar, General Harkabi, writing in the Israeli newspaper *Maariv*, in 1973, said:

> We must define our position and lay down basic principles for a settlement. Our demands should be moderate and balanced, and appear to be reasonable. But in fact they must involve such conditions as to ensure that the enemy rejects them. Then we should manoeuvre and allow him to define his own position, and reject a settlement on the basis of a compromise solution. We should then publish his demands as embodying unreasonable extremism.

Israel is the only democracy in the Middle East
The first thing to note is that Turkey would generally be regarded as being in the Middle East and Lebanon and Jordan certainly so.

Is Israel a democracy? One might ask: how can a nation that denies a vote to four million people in lands that it totally controls (and doesn't contemplate giving up) describe itself as a democracy? Non-Jewish people born in the Occupied Territories have no rights to Israeli nationality. Jewish people so born do, as do Jews born anywhere in the world. This is not democracy. For democracy to exist there must be equality before the law for all citizens.

If one looks only at Israel proper there is not even such equality.

Of all the land that may be legally sold in Israel, 67 per cent of it may not legally be sold to Arab citizens; there are no restrictions on land sales to Jewish citizens. Israeli Arabs are second-class Israeli citizens. Within pre-'67 Israel, 93 per cent of land was reserved as a national land trust or Jewish National Fund land. It is for the exclusive use of Jews. The 20 per cent of the population that is Palestinian living in Israel have to share access to the remaining 7 per cent of private land.[12]

Further, Arab towns and villages have fewer internal resources, and receive much less financial assistance from common central budgets, only 3 to 5 per cent of the total. Arab towns have pot-holed roads without sidewalks, no public spaces, no private lawns, overcrowding, and children playing in the streets for lack of playgrounds.[13]

Then we turn to the Occupied Territories. How can there be democracy there? And even if within Israel proper there was a true democracy the consensus of that democracy cannot determine what it will do to a foreign population.

Ilan Pappe has described Israel as a herrenvolk democracy; democracy only for the masters, for one ethnic group, which, given the space Israel controls, i.e. including the Territories, is not even a majority group. No known definition of democracy applies to Israel.

Adalah, the Legal Centre for Minority Rights in Israel, counts more than 35 Israeli laws explicitly privileging Jews over non-Jews. Other Israeli laws appear neutral, but are applied in discriminatory fashion. For example, laws facilitating government land seizures make no reference to Palestinians, but nonetheless have been used almost exclusively to expropriate their properties for Jewish settlements.

Consider the position in Australia if our Constitution defined us as a 'Christian democratic state', our law barred marriage across ethnic-religious lines, our government appointed a Chief Priest empowered to define membership criteria for the Christian nation, our government invited all Christians anywhere in the world to become citizens but barred all others, and our government funded a Centre for Demography that worked to increase the birth rates of Christians to ensure majority status.

CHAPTER 12
Australia

Australian governments of both persuasions have a record of blind support to the State of Israel. That might be considered a defensible policy if Israel had been a state that evidenced a desire to arrive at an honest and reasonable accommodation with the indigenous peoples of Palestine. That has not however been Israel's history, at the very least not since 1988.

Australia had a reasonable record in its stance against apartheid in South Africa. The apartheid regime in South Africa never treated its black population as the Israelis have treated the Palestinians. It never sent F16s to bomb them; it never, systematically, adopted policies that brought the black population to economic and social collapse and despair.

On 19 January 2003, Greg Sheridan giving his Middle East Report in the *Australian*, wrote:

> Australia's national identity and strategic orientation are never hedged or obfuscated in the Middle East. Australia stands four square as one of the strongest and most reliable of US allies, as much in the Middle East as any where else in the World, as the Iraq war illustrates.
>
> Moreover, Australia is also one of the strongest and most reliable friends of Israel in the Western World. The resurgent anti-Semitism that so disfigures the politics of Western Europe has been substantially absent from Australia.

In other words, we toe the line. We fulfil our role as the US puppet. Mr Sheridan is painfully correct.

The referral to the International Court of Justice seeking an advisory opinion on the legal consequences of Israeli construction of the wall on occupied Palestinian land has been addressed.[1] The vote against the referral by Australia was accompanied by no internal debate in this country – indeed, it passed virtually without comment in the Australian media. When the Reverend Dr Alan Reid sought an explanation for the vote from the Department of Foreign Affairs, he received a letter from the Director of the Middle East Section (dated 22.1.04) giving the following reason:

> Australia voted against the United Nations General Assembly resolution seeking an International Court of Justice opinion on the legal consequences of Israel's barrier because we do not believe that there is benefit to be gained from involving the International Court of Justice in the Israeli–Palestinian dispute.

That's it? What does that tell us about the level of thinking in our government? The author has been a practising lawyer for 40 years. In that time he has never heard it suggested that a court is an inappropriate arena in which to air or seek to resolve disputes.

On 1 December 2006 Australia voted 'No' with Israel, the US and four small Pacific island states to the UN General Assembly resolutions re-affirming the inalienable rights of the Palestinian people to self-determination and an independent state; 157 states voted in favour.

The only diversion in this commitment, by Australia, occurred in November 2012 when Australia abstained on the status of Palestine vote. Many would say that it is bad enough that Australia abstained, but given the opposition of then Prime Minister Julia Gillard, the event demonstrated at least a preparedness of members of the Labor caucus to challenge orthodoxy.

The *Australian* newspaper, solidly behind Israel in all respects, reported that this was the only clear instance on record of Gillard being thwarted by her Cabinet and caucus. The revolt was led by then Foreign Minister Carr. Labor MP Michael Danby, an Australian Jew, took out a newspaper advertisement in his seat in the recent election distancing himself from his own foreign minister – dual loyalty?

The Coalition, Australia's then conservative opposition government, was critical of the Gillard government's position at the UN and made it clear that they would have voted against. As Ross Burns (former Australian Ambassador to Israel) pointed out, Australia's position has shifted, 'quietly', without being communicated to the public, to a more pro-Israeli one. At least that was the position until the abstention in November 2012.

The prior commitment to a viable Palestine has apparently been abandoned. Australia avoids any criticism of new Israeli settlement activity on the West Bank. Is it any wonder that we are caught up in the so-called War on Terror as a major player and a target?

In May 2007, John Howard and the *Australian*'s Greg Sheridan were rewarded with the Jerusalem Prize. Howard has a forest in the Negev named after him, a forest that now displaces the indigenous Bedouin Arabs who have lived there since the beginning of time. How hypocritical we are. Australian tax dollars are used to support the Jewish National Fund, a fund used to cleanse the land of Palestine of its Arab ownership. Such was the claim of Dr Uri Davis, Israeli Jewish academic, who came to Australia in 2005 and addressed the National Press Club. It was a claim put to the Australian Tax Office and not as yet refuted.

An example of the extent to which the Australian government is influenced by Israel is the commemorative issue of two stamps in May 2013 marking the battle of Beersheba in 1917, which preceded the capture of Jerusalem by General Allenby. The stamps suggest that this (the battle) was a joint venture between Israel and Australia – and Australia somehow becomes part of the Zionist narrative of the return to Israel. As Israel did not come into existence until 1948 and as any local support to Australian forces was overwhelmingly Arab it is not difficult to see how Palestinians and Palestinian supporters would have been offended. That support was constituted by the harrying of Turkish supply lines by Arab attacks on the Hejaz railway, and by the protection thus afforded on the Australian forces' eastern flank. It is highlighted by the fact that Faisal's army was placed under Allenby's direct command.

Readers might allow the author a small indulgence at this point. In January 1941, a world war later, and still before Israel came into existence, Sergeant Del Smith of the Australian Second 7th Division left Woodside, South Australia. He was in fact part of re-enforcements to the Division, which had left on 17 November 1940. Smith, a gunner with the regiment's 13th Battery, travelled aboard the troopship *Mauritania*. He continues his story:

> The *Mauritania* was a brand new ship. It had 5000 troops on board. The *Queen Mary* was in the convoy. Other ships were waiting south of Tasmania. We met them there, the *Queen Mary*, *Aquitania* and another ship. There was only one escort, the *Gloucester*. Then we went to Perth. The *Mauritania* went in and we picked up the Western Australians. We had five to six hours leave.

From there we went on to Bombay. The *Queen Mary* went on to Singapore and nearly all of those troops were taken. We had three weeks at Bombay. Actually it was called Deolali, about 150 miles north of Bombay. It was a staging camp. We drilled. It was a permanent British Army camp which reinforced troops at the Khyber Pass. This was my first time out of the country.

From there we went on through the Red Sea. We changed ships because of the guns in Italian Somalia. I was on the *New Zealand*. We were put off about 25 miles from Port Said. There we went into Palestine. We were there for five months. Qastina camp was one – the other was on the way towards Gaza. Jerusalem was three to four hours run in a bus. I also had two to three days in Tel Aviv. We stayed at the King David Hotel in Jerusalem. When we went to the Holy Sepulchre we could see the Wailing Wall.

The brigade saw service in Lebanon, Syria, and later Libya. Sergeant Smith only participated in Libya. Sergeant Delbridge Heywood Smith was the author's father. In 1998, a year before his death, the author took an oral history from his father, a portion of which has been reproduced.

Qastina was a Palestinian village in territory allotted to the Arab state under the 1947 UN Partition Plan. As such, it can be assumed that the village was totally inhabited by Arabs. In the event those local people who supported the Australian forces at Qastina with necessary services were Arab. Again, it is to be expected that Palestinians would be offended by the commemorative stamp.

The ancient Palestinian city of Beersheba was also allocated to the Arabs in the Partition Plan. As with Qastina the Arab inhabitants fled in the 1948 war. They have never been allowed to return to their homes.

On 9 July 1948 the village of Qastina and its over 147 houses were completely destroyed by Israeli forces after its inhabitants fled. The village thereafter ceased to exist. Today there are four Israeli localities on the lands of the former village: Kfar Warburg, Arugot, Kfar Ahim, and Kiryat Malakhi.[2]

The occupation ought to be the number one foreign policy issue facing Australia today. Many Australians know this truth already. Their vote needs to be directed. The peace process, rather than leading to a solution, exacerbates the occupation. The longer this so-called even-handed process continues, the more it disadvantages Palestinians as the occupation expands and becomes more entrenched, and the less likely it is to have a meaningful outcome. The first step to peace is an end to the 45-year occupation.

The views expressed here are not extreme. They represent the thinking of the vast majority of the Community of Nations. Former Australian prime ministers Malcolm Fraser and Bob Hawke have, at least in recent times, expressed similar views.

On 7 September 2013, a new conservative government was elected. It boded ill for people of goodwill who want to see Australia take a positive step in the resolution of this conflict, particularly as Australia is to take up the position of Presidency of the Security Council.

In the days preceding the September 2013 election, the Foreign Minister and deputy leader of the party, Julie Bishop, attacked the Greens over its supposed 'support' of the Boycott Divestment Sanctions (BDS) movement. Bishop demanded that (the Greens leader) Senator Milne clarify her party's stand on 'the anti-Semitic boycott, divestment and sanctions campaign'. To so describe the BDS campaign demonstrates a remarkable lack of understanding by an incoming foreign minister. The writer quotes from the Australians for BDS call for support:

> The BDS movement is a call for justice by all sectors of Palestinian civil society and supported around the world by unions, churches, civil society and human rights groups. It is a form of non-violent popular resistance and international solidarity in protest against Israel's persistent violation of Palestinian human rights and international law.
>
> BDS policies make it clear that it is a human rights based movement and opposed to racism in all forms, including anti-Semitism.

Inspired by the effective movement against apartheid South Africa, BDS is directed against the illegal military occupation and settlements of the West Bank, the collective punishment of Gaza and Israeli discrimination of its own Palestinian citizens.

BDS opposes corporations, institutions and organisations which support Israel's violation of human rights and international law including businesses such as Caterpillar, Motorola, G4S and Veolia.

On 14 November 2013 Australia voted against four motions in the Fourth Committee of the United Nations General Assembly that condemned activities of Israel as the occupying power of the Occupied Palestine Territories.

Inter alia the motions condemned those policies and practices of Israel, which violated the human rights of the Palestinian people and expressed grave concern about the critical situation in the Occupied Palestinian Territories, including East Jerusalem, and particularly in the Gaza Strip, as a result of unlawful Israeli practices and measures particularly illegal settlement.

The motions were overwhelmingly carried; Australia, Canada, Federated States of Micronesia, Israel, Nauru, Palau, Panama and the United States voted against.

Such a vote by Australia is a clear departure from the position of the prior Labor government. The votes were not publicised in Australia nor were they the subject of discussion or public debate.

CHAPTER 13

A Resolution?

Paul Findley from Illinois was a member of the US Congress for 22 years. He was a Republican. On 27 January 2003 he spoke in Congress.

> The President's best war decision is purely a political one, and it is plain, peaceful, generous and just. He must make a clean break from Israel's scofflaw behaviour. If Bush has the will, he can easily free himself and America. If he acts, he will transform the grim scene in Iraq and elsewhere in the Middle East into bright promise. Any day he chooses, the President can instantly – without firing a shot – quiet guerrilla warfare in Iraq and anti-American protests throughout the World.
>
> All he needs do is inform Sharon that all aid will be suspended until Israel vacates the Arab territory Israeli forces seized in June 1967. US aid is literally Israel's lifeline, so the ultimatum would be electrifying evidence that the United States, at long last, will do what is right for Arabs and Muslims. (I interpose to remind that only about one fifth of the one sixth of mankind who are Muslims are Arabs.) If Bush acts, the Iraqi people will have reason to believe, for the first time, that the US government truly opposes colonialism.
>
> The ultimatum would prompt rejoicing worldwide, not just among Iraqis and Palestinians. Opinion polls show that a large majority of Israelis, weary of the long, bloody struggle to subjugate the Palestinians, would welcome co-existence with an independent, peaceful Palestine.
>
> An impressive foundation for this presidential ultimatum already exists. All member-states of the Arab League unanimously offered peace-for-withdrawal four years ago. A similar plan called the Geneva Accords was recently announced jointly by former

officials of Israel and Palestine. Almost simultaneously, four retired heads of Israeli intelligence even urged full, unilateral withdrawal from the West Bank and Gaza.

By standing resolutely for justice for Palestinians, who are mostly Muslim, Bush would virtually end anti-American protests and strengthen moderate forces worldwide.

Edward Said in *The End of the Peace Process* asserts:

> I have no doubt that the only acceptable form of peace between Israel and Palestine must really be a mutual one, in which Israel cannot enjoy benefits like sovereignty, security, territorial continuity, real political independence, and national self-determination, and Palestine not. Peace must be between equals, which is exactly what is wrong with the Oslo peace process ... in none of the hundreds of pages of texts ... is there any indication that Palestinians would have the right to sovereignty, or that Israel would completely remove its army and settlements of occupation.

Many suggest that the world today is in the mess it is in because of this one running sore: the injustice done to the Palestinian people. Some will say that this is to overstate the significance of Palestine. The writer however advances the suggestion.

Palestine has affected the view of the Arab world towards the West in a totally understandable way. Peter Mansfield, in *The Arabs* (1976), records a conversation with an intelligent and sensitive Palestinian who worked for the Arab League and was therefore familiar with all the Arab states. The usual US–Israeli thesis that Arab governments only use the Palestinians as a convenient diversion from their own domestic problems was put to him. Mansfield records:

> His reply was categorical. Palestine was in the heart and mind of every Arab wherever he was living. It was the first thing he thought about in the morning and the last thing at night.

The same issue is forefront in the emotions of all Muslims. The arrogant actions of the settlers towards the inhabitants of the

Occupied Territories are a constant humiliation and exacerbation of their feelings. For the sake of 450,000 settlers illegally occupying Arab lands the world is held to ransom. But the West insists on looking for causes anywhere but Palestine.

Since 9/11 the West has conducted a war on terrorism. But we are not allowed to ask what might be the causes of terrorism. Any policeman, confronted by a crime, looks for a motive. But the US and Israel do not want people to question what the settlers are doing in the Occupied Territories and whether it might be a root cause of terrorism. If that were considered, people might suggest that the occupation should end.

It is appropriate to consider 'The 9/11 Commission Report'. There is an almost complete failure by the Commission to seriously consider why the event occurred. This failure renders the work almost completely useless. No doubt there are some useful analyses of response capacities, and so on. However the American people, who were entitled to have some attempt made at an explanation, were short-changed.

Television news reports on the day of publication of the Report asserted that numerous people were expressing astonishment at the almost total lack of reference to Palestine. These people were not hard-core liberals, leftists, or socialists. Rather, they were people who had given evidence to the commission, persons from the CIA and State Department, who had testified to the fact that, when questioning persons associated with those involved in the attack, they had almost invariably cited the injustices perpetrated upon the Palestinian people, and the US's unquestioning support of Israel in the infliction of those injustices, as the prime motivation for a violent attempt to bring that anger to the awareness of the American public.

This criticism of their report was put to a couple of the commissioners whose response was 'Well, Israel is an ally of this country'. One might ask the purpose of the commission if not to present the facts.

There are 428 pages in the substantive report. Ten pages have reference to Israel, most of which are peripheral. The elephant in the room is almost totally ignored.[1]

When the commission turns its mind to 'What To Do? A Global Strategy', it makes 28 recommendations over 38 pages. Not one is addressed to the US policy on Israel and resolution of the Palestinian issue. Not one is addressed to bringing the 'peace process' to an end. If there had been one such recommendation, which was implemented, the other 28 may not have been necessary.

⚜

There is an international campaign to isolate Israel in sport, commerce, academia and the arts until Israel complies with the norms of a civilised nation. That is the BDS Movement. This boycotting is appropriate. After all it was the Zionists who introduced the boycott into the contest. The kibbutz movement at the beginning of the last century led to the expulsion of Arab labour and, as soon as the Jews could produce enough of their own, to the boycott of Arab goods. From the first expulsion of an Arab labourer from a Jewish farm, the Zionists set in train a reaction that has resulted in an Arab blockade of Israel. The State of Israel has been trying to break out of that quarantine since its birth. It is still doing so.

The recent EU directive to its members to exclude West Bank settlements from any future deals with Israel is notable. It forbids any funding, co-operation, scholarships, research funds or prizes to anyone residing in the Jewish settlements in the West Bank and East Jerusalem. This presents a clear and unambiguous position that the EU believes Israel's borders are those prior to 1967. If the EU and others still holding out do not recognise a State of Palestine within its full pre-1967 borders, there seems strong reason for the Palestinians to return to the UN and press them to do so.

The writer quotes, finally, again from Edward Said in *The End of the Peace Process*:

If every one of us first took it upon him/herself to be informed about what people in Ramallah or Hebron or Bethlehem or Jerusalem are going through, and then attempted somehow to break through the official and media silence – a letter to the editor, a call to a radio or TV station, the setting up of groups to do this kind of work systematically and collectively – then we will be beginning our attempt at liberation, a miniscule and even laughably modest attempt, it is true, but surely a great deal better than passivity and collective silence.

The resolution is simple. The Security Council calls upon Israel to cease its occupation of the Occupied Territories – all of it: no negotiations, no 'agreed land swaps'. Israel has had ample time to agree land swaps if it wanted them. It didn't.

Upon the failure of Israel to cease its occupation, sanctions will be imposed. The world will readily embrace them. Israel is only too aware of the consequences of holding out. It will comply. If it doesn't, a UN force must be deployed to isolate it, and to secure the West Bank, and the territorial integrity of Gaza.

It is necessary to now turn to the difficult issue of the end game. There can never be reconciliation and acceptance to a final status dictated by one party. Nor will it avail Israel to have a signature by the current Palestinian Authority, which so clearly does not represent the Palestinian people.

There is a need to undo the wrong, not just of 1967, but of 1947–1948. The undoing of that wrong must concentrate upon the right of return recognised by the General Assembly of the United Nations on 11 December 1948. People must be allowed to return to their homes. 'People' in this context must include the second and third and fourth generations. Nor should it be suggested that this would be too difficult to administer. If Spain feels confident that it can identify the descendants of Jews expelled in the 15th century – 600 years ago – so that their descendants can return, Israel/Palestine must surely be able to do so after only 60 years.

But it cannot be a one-way fix. Jewish people uprooted, in one way or another, from their homes in Iran, Germany, Morocco, Egypt or Greece, must have the same right of return – a right of return to communities from which they were either driven or enticed.

So too must their desire to remain in Israel, or, indeed, Palestine, be respected.

Whether the two nations of Israel and Palestine decide in ten, or 20, or 30 years to become one nation will be a matter for the citizens at that time. Much will no doubt depend upon the success of a truth and reconciliation commission such as that implemented in South Africa to heal that divided nation.

There would appear to be no alternative.

Epilogue

Let us return to the Dreyfus affair.

On 13 January 1898 Emile Zola published in *L'Aurore* his timeless 'J'Accuse'. It is a unique document. The essay addressed publicly the President of the Republic and assails the anti-Semitic prejudice of French society. Zola asserts:

> My duty is to speak; I have no wish to be an accomplice. My nights would be haunted by the spectre of the innocent being, expiating under the most frightful torture, a crime he never committed.
>
> General Billot and General Boisdeffre never doubted that the bordereau was the work of Esterhazy; ... (b)ut the ... condemnation of Esterhazy involved ... the revision of the Dreyfus verdict and it was this of all things that the General Staff wished to avoid at all cost ... they cannot permit the innocence of Dreyfus to be recognised without having the whole War Ministry demolished by public wrath ... This then, Mr President, is the Esterhazy affair: a guilty man who had to be exculpated for 'reasons of state'...
>
> But this letter is long, Mr President, and it is time to conclude.
>
> 'J'accuse' General Mercier of having made himself an accomplice in one of the greatest crimes of history, probably through weak-mindedness ...
>
> 'J'accuse' General de Boisdeffre and General Gonse of being accomplices in the same crime, the former no doubt through religious prejudice, the latter through esprit de corps.
>
> 'J'accuse' the War Office of having led a vile campaign in the press ... in order to misdirect public opinion and cover up its sins ...
>
> In making these accusations I am aware that I render myself liable to articles 30 and 31 of the Libel Laws ... I expose myself voluntarily.

In many French cities mobs roamed the streets sacking Jewish stores and desecrating synagogues in the days after 'J'Accuse'. Nevertheless, truth ultimately prevailed, Zola bringing to him other men and women of substance, including Clemenceau, Proust, Peguy and Georges Sorel.

Who is the Emile Zola of 2013? Who stands up to say '*J'accuse*' to the State of Israel? Who says: 'Israel, you are a racist state; Israel, you are guilty of racist acts against the Palestinians'?

Well, there are many: we shall come to them. But we should not single out Israel. We should not forget the accomplices. Who will say: '*J'accuse* the United States of America of racism against the Palestinians'?

Who will say: '*J'accuse* the United Kingdom of racism against the Palestinians'?

Who will say: '*J'accuse* Canada ... *J'accuse* France ... *J'accuse* Australia ...'?

How many Emile Zolas do we need?

We have Nelson Mandela in the *Wall St Journal*, 19 June 1990:

> We are in the same trench struggling against the same enemy: the twin Tel Aviv and Pretoria regimes, apartheid, racism, colonialism and neo-colonialism.

We have Desmond Tutu in his letter to the divestment sponsors at the University of California, April 2010:

> I have witnessed the systemic humiliation of Palestinian men, women and children by members of the Israeli security forces. Their humiliation is familiar to all black South Africans who were corralled and harassed and insulted and assaulted by the security forces of the apartheid government.

We have Noam Chomsky: *Hegemony or Survival*, 2004.

We have Edward Said: *Zionism from the Standpoint of its Victims*, 1979.

We have Ilan Pappe: *The Ethnic Cleansing of Palestine*, 2006; *Out of the Frame*, 2010.

Consider the many.

Postscript

Whilst in Israel for the funeral of Ariel Sharon, Australia's Foreign Minister Julie Bishop made news by declaring Australia would like to see which international law made settlements in Occupied Palestine illegal. Such statements contradict up to 50 years of international consensus in the United Nations General Assembly, the Security Council, and, as we have seen, the International Court of Justice's decision of 2004.

That an Australian government would put at nought a decision of the International Court of Justice, particularly one of such near unanimity, seems remarkable.

When pressed on the issue, Bishop fell back on the somewhat naïve view that the settlements must be a matter of negotiation. Apparently the present Australian government cannot see that 'negotiation' (*sic*) has failed for over 40 years and the reason is obvious – the negotiating parties are wholly unequal and one of them, the stronger, is not interested in a settlement.

Australians deserve better than this from their foreign minister.

⚙

In July 2014, when this book was nearing completion, I was travelling. On 8 July I left New York City for Berlin. On 25 July I left Paris to return to Australia. This sounds ordinary; it's what people do in the 21st century, especially reasonably well-off Australians. But there was something particular about those two to three weeks. They represent a low point in humanity.

On 8 July, the Israel Defense Forces (IDF) launched Operation Protective Edge against militants in the Gaza Strip. This obscenity was, in a strange way, compounded by the shooting down of Malaysian Airlines flight MH17 over Ukraine on 17 July. The two events have left me in despair. What are we leaving our children and grandchildren?

Travelling in foreign countries and not being fluent in their languages meant that the news reports were broken and inaccessible. Often, I didn't have the heart to go to the internet. The *Economist* on 26 July spoke of Putin and 'A web of lies' (concerning MH17). There was no mention of Barack Obama and a web of lies when Obama repeated the mantra: 'Israel has a right to defend itself.' As I hope I have made clear, this is a lie. As the International Court found in 2004, Israel is an occupying power. It remains the occupying power of Gaza as it controls exit and entry by air, land and sea, and access to water, electricity and other fundamentals of life.

Israel cannot both occupy Gaza, and thus usurp the governing powers of its occupants, and at the same time make war upon the Palestinians who live – if that is the right word – there.

Israel simply cannot invoke the right to self-defence as defined in Article 51 of the UN Charter. An armed attack that would justify the invoking of Article 51 must be attributable to a sovereign state. Gaza is not a sovereign state, neither is Hamas nor the launchers of the rockets. Israel must address such activity as an occupier, pursuant to the laws applicable to an occupier, and not pursuant to the laws of war.

Neither can President Obama invoke Article 51. He knows it.

As for the Palestinians living in Gaza, they have a right to resist, by force, an illegal occupation. The firing of rockets is all that is left to them.

Operation Protective Edge is not, at the time of writing, over. I have not written of the deaths, the destruction, the dissolution of civil society. I don't believe I need to.

A final statement. The Jewish people, rightly, came out of World War II with the goodwill of the world. The state of Israel and those who support it, have, however, in my opinion, used up that goodwill.

Paul Heywood-Smith

27 July 2014

Acknowledgements

I acknowledge the support of my wife Edie Bransbury. Edie has tested my theories in conversation and sometimes prevailed.

I acknowledge the valued criticism of my close friend Pete Pierce of the University of Oklahoma, Norman. Pete it was who knocked the rough edges off the original text resulting from my lack of religious study.

I acknowledge too the assistance of Professor Lawrence Davidson of West Chester University Pennsylvania who kindly read the manuscript and proffered invaluable advice.

I acknowledge Jeanie Lucas for her assistance with the original lectures and for her investigative skills in finding and securing photographic materials. Jeanie also provided invaluable criticism on the text.

I also acknowledge the proofreading of both Edie and my daughter Emily.

Notes

Chapter 1 – Ancient History and Religion

1 Sand, *The Invention of the Land of Israel*, p. 130.
2 Verso, 2009.
3 Per Chief Justice Mason and Justice McHugh at (*No. 2*) p. 15.

Chapter 2 – The 7th to the 19th Century

1 I acknowledge the work of Shlomo Sand referred to in this paragraph, at pp. 27–28.
2 Phoenix, 2011.
3 W.S. Holdsworth, *A History of English Law*, Methuen & Co. Ltd, 1903, Vol. I, pp. 45–46.
4 *Commentaries on the Laws of England*, Vol. 4, p. 59.
5 W.S. Holdsworth, above, Vol. VIII, pp. 406–410.
6 *Commentaries*, above, Vol. 4, p. 365.
7 *The Complete Diaries of Theodore Herzl*, Herzl Press and Thomas Yoseloff, NY, 1960, Vol. I, p. 88.

Chapter 3 – Early 20th Century and the Balfour Declaration

1 D. Hirst, *The Gun and the Olive Branch*, Nation Books, 2003, p. 159.
2 Doubleday, 2013, p. 271.
3 Cornelius John, *The Hidden History of the Balfour Declaration*, Washington Report on Middle East Affairs, November 2005.
4 Hirst, above, p. 179.

Chapter 4 – Resistance to Nakba

1 Photo, p. 28.
2 Hirst, above, p. 171.
3 Lilienthal, *What Price Israel?* (2004), citing *So Far So Good* by Morris L. Ernst, Harper, 1948, pp. 170–177.

4 McKeenin, *The Berlin–Baghdad Express*, Penguin, 2010, p. 362.

5 Hirst, above, pp. 238–239.

6 N. Chomsky, *The Fateful Triangle, The US, Israel and the Palestinians*, Cambridge, MA: South End Press, 1999. 'In internal discussion in 1938 Ben Gurion stated that "after we become a strong force, as a result of the creation of a state, we shall abolish partition and expand into the whole of Palestine".'

7 UN Transcripts, 29 September 1947.

8 Hirst, above, pp. 256–257.

9 A. Weir, *Against our Better Judgment, The hidden history of how the United States was used to create Israel*, April 2013.

10 Truman Library, Abraham Feinberg Oral History Interview.

11 W. Eveland, *Ropes of Sand: America's failure in the Middle East*, London, 1980.

12 Hirst, above, pp. 278–279.

13 Hirst, above, pp. 248–250.

14 Dugard, *The Secession of States and Their Recognition in the Wake of Kosovo*, Hague Academy of International Law, 2013, p. 187, citing Crawford.

15 Sir Raphael Cilento was the father of the well-known Australian actress Diane Cilento.

16 De Waal, *The Hare with Amber Eyes*, Chatto & Windus, 2010, p. 109.

17 F. Jerome, *Einstein on Zionism and Israel: His Provocative Ideas About the Middle East*. St Martin's Press, 2009.

18 I. Deutscher, *The Prophet Outcast*, Oxford, 1963, p. 369.

Chapter 5 – 1948 to 1967 and the pre-1967 US/Israeli Relationship

1 Allen & Unwin, 2002.

2 Mearsheimer & Walt, *The Israel Lobby*, Farrar, Straus and Giroux, 2007, p. 99.

3 T. Segev, *The June '67 War and the Palestinian Refugee Problem*, University of California Press, 2013.

4 Stephen Green, *Taking Sides, America's Secret Relations with a Militant Israel, 1948/1967*, Faber, 1984, pp. 150–154.

5 Stephen Green, above, at pp. 205, 206.

6 The *Liberty* incident is referenced to Stephen Green, *Taking Sides*, above.

Chapter 6 – 1967 to the 21st Century

1 Segev, above.

2 Baltzer, *Witness in Palestine*, Paradigm Publishing, 2007, p. 385.

Chapter 7 – The Wall and the International Court of Justice

1 No. IV: Respecting the Laws and Customs of War on Land, 1907.

2 2013.

3 The writer acknowledges the paper by Sam Blay in 78 ALJ 710.

Chapter 8 – The 2006 Lebanese War

1 Oslo 2, refer above.

Chapter 9 – The US/Israeli Relationship – Part 2

1 Nathan-Kazis, *The Jewish Charity Industry Uncovered*, 24 March 2014.

2 Mitchell Bard was the former editor of AIPAC's (American Israel Public Affairs Committee) *Near East Report*.

3 Ezekial, xxxvii, 21.

4 Evangelists comprise Baptists (literal Calvinists) and faith healing Pentecostals (e.g. Assembly of God). These two groups ally politically but detest each other, as much as they jointly detest Roman Catholics.

5 Rabkin, *A Threat from Within: A Century of Jewish Opposition to Zionism*, Zed Books, 2006, p. 150.

6 Gorenberg, *The End of Days*, Oxford Univ. Press, 2000, p. 166.

7 Lawrence Davidson, *What National Interest? An Analysis*, 5 August 2013.

8 Op cit.

9 *Guardian Weekly*, 20–26 September 2013.

10 Pew Research, *Religion & Public Life Project*, 1 October 2013.

11 *Zionism versus Diplomacy and Peace – An Analysis*, 5 September 2013.

Chapter 10 – Today

1 *Guardian Weekly*, 16 August 2013, asserts that Ateret Cohanim, the organisation behind the yeshiva in the Muslim Quarter is funded by benefactors such as Irving Moscowitz, an octogenarian US bingo tycoon.

2 Amira Hass writing in *Haaretz* in September 2010.

3 Prof. Mark Levine, Lund University, Sweden, commenting upon the Goldstone Report in November 2009.

Chapter 11 – Myths and Other Issues

1 Reprinted in *The Edward Said Reader*, Vintage Books, 2000.
2 p. 95.
3 *Times of Israel*, 9 September 2013.
4 6 March 2008, p. 30.
5 Reinhart, *Israel/Palestine*, Allen & Unwin, 2002, p. 116.
6 Footnote 8.
7 Morgan Jayton, *The Theology of Government Shutdown: Christian dominionism*, 1 October 2013.
8 Amanda Marrotte, *Christian delusions are driving the GOP insane*, 10 October 2013.
9 Professor Lawrence Davidson, *Ideological Disaster – An Analysis*, 20 October 2013.
10 Refer Chapter 9.
11 Hirst, p. 139.
12 Dr Hatim Kanaaheh, *Shattering the Myth of Democracy and Equality in Israel*: 6 April 2009 – [11].
13 *Ibid.*

Chapter 12 – Australia

1 Chapter 7.
2 Palestine Remembered, retrieved 12 March 2007.

Chapter 13 – A Resolution?

1 The ten pages are pp. 51, 56, 61, 147, 250, 256, 257, 259, 260 and 362.

Sources

(Excluding newspaper and periodical materials.)

England and Palestine, Herbert Sidebotham, Constable, 1918.

The Jewish Problem, Louis Golding, Penguin, 1938.

Mandate Memories, 1918–1948, Norman and Helen Bentwich, The Hogarth Press, 1965.

The Thirteenth Tribe, Arthur Koestler, Hutchinson, 1976.

The Arabs, Peter Mansfield, Pelican, 1978.

Taking Sides, America's Secret Relations with a Militant Israel, 1948/1967, Stephen Green, Faber, 1984.

The Israel–Arab Reader, Walter Laqueur and Barry Rubin, Pelican, 1984.

The Penguin History of the World, J.M. Roberts, Penguin, 1995.

The Edward Said Reader, Moustafa Bayoumi and Andrew Rubin (eds), Vintage Books, NY, 2000.

The End of Days, Fundamentalism and the Struggle for the Temple Mount, Gershom Gorenberg, Oxford, 2000.

The End of the Peace Process, Edward Said, Granta, 2002.

The Gun and the Olive Branch, David Hirst, Nation Books, 2003.

Israel/Palestine, Tanya Reinhart, Allen & Unwin, 2003.

The Case for Israel, Alan Dershowitz, Wiley, 2003.

Dishonest Broker: The US Role in Israel and Palestine, Naseer H. Aruri, South End Press, 2003.

A History of Modern Palestine, Ilan Pappe, Cambridge UP, 2004.

The Great War for Civilization, Robert Fisk, Fourth Estate, 2005.

Palestine, Peace Not Apartheid, Jimmy Carter, Simon & Schuster, 2006.

Failing Peace, Sarah Roy, Pluto Press, 2007.

The Israel Lobby and US Foreign Policy, Mearsheimer and Walt, Farrar, 2007.

Witness in Palestine, Anna Baltzer, Paradigm Publishers, 2007.

The Invention of the Jewish People, Shlomo Sand, Verso, 2009.

The Modern Middle East, 2nd edn, Ilan Pappe, Routledge, 2010.

Out of the Frame, Ilan Pappe, Pluto Press, 2010.

Israel Palestine, Craig Nielsen, Adelaide, 2010.

The Berlin-Baghdad Express, Sean McMeekin, Penguin, 2010.

Jerusalem, Simon Montefiore, Phoenix, 2011.

The Forgotten Palestinians, Ilan Pappe, Yale UP, 2011.

The Invention of the Land of Israel, Shlomo Sand, Verso, 2012.

Lawrence in Arabia, Scott Anderson, Doubleday, 2013.

Index

[Bold numbers in brackets refer to Figure numbers]

Church of the Holy Sepulchre 12, 24
Church of the Nativity 16
Cilento, Sir Raphael 40, 41, [7]
Clifford, Clark 38
Clinton, Bill 54–56, 58, 77, 79, 80
Cold War 76
Constantine 7, 30
Constantinople 8
Cressor, Warder 78
Crimean War 16, 27
Crocker, Sir Walter 40, 41, [10]
Crusades 10, 14

D
Damascus 23, 26, 39
Danby, Michael 107
Davidson, Professor Lawrence 81, 83
Davis, Dr Uri 108
Deir Yassin 39
Democratic Party 49
dhimmi tax 12
Dimona 50
Disraeli, Benjamin 17 [1]
Dome of the Rock 12, 15
Dreyfus 17, 18, 23, 119, [2]

E
East Jerusalem 56–58, 66, 75, 85, 86, 88
Eastern Church 8
Eder, Dr 28
Edict of Milan 7
Edward I 22
Egypt 10, 16, 17, 26, 27, 33, 47, 48, 53, 85, 99, 118
Einstein, Albert 43, 44
Eisenhower, Dwight 48, 50
Eliot, George 27
Elon, Amos 53

Emir Hussein 26
Ernst, Morris 36
Esterhazy 18, 119
Ethiopia 61
Eveland, Wilbur 38

F
Faisal 26, 108
Falk, Richard 81
Falwell, Jerry 79
Fatah 48, 69, 100
Feinberg, Abraham 38
Ferdinand and Isabella 15
Findley, Paul 113
First Temple 6
France 15, 17, 18, 26, 27, 48, 50, 76, 120
Frankfurter, Felix 49
Franks 10, 14
Fraser, Malcolm 111
Frederick II 14

G
Galerius 7
Gaza 30, 47, 49, 51, 53, 55, 57, 58, 69, 70–72, 75, 84, 85, 87, 89, 100, 112, 117, 121, 122
General Assembly, *see* United Nations General Assembly
Geneva Convention, Fourth 62, 65, 66, 75, 87
Germany 4, 13, 25, 36, 38, 40, 44, 48, 118
Gillard, Julia 84, 107, 108
Gilo 100
Gingrich, Newt 82
Golan Heights 48, 51, 70, 71, 75, 76
Goldstein, Baruch 99
Goldstone Report 89
Gorenberg, Gershom 79

Index

Index

Wakefield Press is an independent publishing and
distribution company based in Adelaide, South Australia.
We love good stories and publish beautiful books.
To see our full range of books, please visit our website at
www.wakefieldpress.com.au
where all titles are available for purchase.

Find us!

Twitter: www.twitter.com/wakefieldpress
Facebook: www.facebook.com/wakefield.press
Instagram: instagram.com/wakefieldpress

www.ingramcontent.com/pod-product-compliance
Lightning Source LLC
Chambersburg PA
CBHW071746270326
41928CB00013B/2816